England's Schools

History, architecture and adaptation

England's Schools

History, architecture and adaptation

Elain Harwood

ENGLISH HERITAGE

Front cover
Sydenham School, London, additions by Basil Spence and Partners, 1957 (see also p 72).
[DP059443]

Inside front cover
Motif from the Corsham Board School (Wilts), 1895.
[DP059576]

Frontispiece
One of the best-known adaptations of a board school is the very successful Ikon Gallery, created in 1998 by Levitt Bernstein Associates from Oozells Street School, Birmingham, 1877–8 by Martin and Chamberlain.
[DSC6666]

Inside back cover
Rugby School (Warwicks) from the air.
[AP26234/010]

Back cover
Bideford Technical Schools (Devon), now the town's arts centre, from 1896. The large size of the plaque in proportion to the building reflects the scale of the municipal pride involved, lost when school boards were abolished in 1902.
[DP082387]

Published by English Heritage, Kemble Drive, Swindon SN2 2GZ
www.english-heritage.org.uk
English Heritage is the Government's statutory adviser on all aspects of the historic environment.

© English Heritage 2010

Images (except as otherwise shown) © English Heritage or © Crown copyright. NMR.

First published 2010

ISBN 9781848020313
Product code 51476

British Library Cataloguing in Publication data
A CIP catalogue record for this book is available from the British Library.

The National Monuments Record is the public archive of English Heritage. For more information, contact NMR Enquiry and Research Services, National Monuments Record Centre, Kemble Drive, Swindon SN2 2GZ; telephone (01793) 414600.

Brought to publication by Joan Hodsdon, Publishing, English Heritage.

Typeset in ITC Charter 9.25 on 13pt
Photographs by Steve Cole, Nigel Corrie, James O Davies, Bob Skingle and Peter Williams
Aerial photographs by Damian Grady and Matt Oakey
Plans redrawn by Nigel Fradgley
Edited by Jan Mitchell
Page layout by Simon Borrough
Printed in the UK by Norwich Colour Print Ltd.

Contents

Acknowledgements

This book grew out of detailed research for English Heritage and the Greater London Council by the following: the late Susan Beattie, and James Douet, Mike Eaton, Keith Miller, Nigel Morgan, Andrew Saint, Pete Smith and Sue Wrathmell. I would particularly like to thank the late David Medd for passing on his experience of post-war school design, an area where further research is being aided by Geraint Franklin. The project was revived by John Cattell. Tim Brennan drafted much of the material for the introduction. Rex Batey, Peter Hoey, Julian Holder, Francis Kelly, Edward Kitchen, Isla MacNeal and Trevor Mitchell helped with case studies, and Susie Barson, Roger Bowdler, Colum Giles and Delcia Keate read the text. The greatest thanks is due to James O Davies, who took many splendid photographs specifically for this book, to Nigel Fradgley for the plans and to Damian Grady and Matt Oakey for aerial photography. Thanks are also due to Jan Mitchell, editor, and Simon Borrough, designer, and to Clare Blick, Joan Hodsdon, John Hudson and Robin Taylor for their advice and contribution to this project.

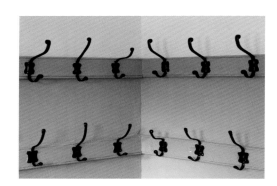

Foreword

Most of us reading this will remember our first school. It is one of the few early experiences in which we can all share. But why was our school the way it was, what informed its shape and style? This book aims to broaden our understanding of the historical and architectural development behind the buildings in which we spent so many of our formative years. It is based on new research, but has grown out of reports commissioned by English Heritage in the 1990s when our schools – particularly those of the 19th century – first began to be recognised for their cultural heritage as well as their architecture. This book brings the story closer to the present time.

Our children deserve the very best learning environment that the education system can offer. This view is reflected in the Government's major programme to rebuild or refurbish England's school buildings over a ten to fifteen year period. No one doubts that there are some school buildings that are no longer suitable as places of education and which must pass into other uses or be demolished. But it is equally clear that there are others which are inherently flexible in their design and planning, and which can and should be refurbished. It is also becoming increasingly apparent, as the question of sustainability assumes an ever greater global relevance, that new does not necessarily mean better. The very best of our existing schools warrant protection as 'listed' buildings in recognition of their architectural and historical significance, their role as local landmarks, and above all their continuing ability to inspire generations of children. English Heritage is adamant that listing should not preclude change, but rather ensure that any alterations are carefully considered and are themselves of high quality.

This book explains why different types of schools look they way they do and sets out the criteria for listing. It also includes some case studies demonstrating that historic school buildings can be successfully refurbished to create superb learning environments. Other case studies show schools put to new uses in the public domain as well as making exciting places to work and live.

Our policy is to encourage local authorities to include consideration of the historic and architectural qualities of school buildings alongside the range of other factors that must be taken into account when deciding whether to demolish or refurbish these structures. In the guidance available via our website (www.helm.org.uk), we encourage authorities to carry out rapid assessments of their school estates to ensure that heritage considerations play a full part in the planning of future school provision. These heritage assessments are best undertaken early on to help provide certainty and to reduce the chances of unforeseen issues arising at a later stage.

English Heritage will continue to work with the Department for Children, Schools and the Family, Partnership for Schools, the Council for Architecture and the Built Environment and other partners to promote recognition of the heritage values of historic school buildings. For it is only by understanding, and appreciating these structures that we can make fully informed decisions about their future. This is the first book in the Informed Conservation series to give a national overview of a major building type. We hope that there is something of interest here for everyone.

Baroness Andrews, Chair of English Heritage

1

Introduction

with Tim Brennan

School was the first experience outside the family environment most of us can remember. Our experiences varied, and the idea of preserving school buildings prompts very different reactions in different people. The schools themselves are similarly diverse, ranging from red-brick Victorian board schools to lightweight structures mainly of glass from the 1950s and 1960s, and some are much older schoolrooms founded by a local charity, church or chapel. But school life is changing. The increasing use of computer technology and a wider range of activities outside school hours have called into question the value of the traditional classroom. The government is investing in the rebuilding or extensive remodelling of many of our schools. Its campaign for secondary schools, 'Building Schools for the Future', was announced in early 2004, and is to be followed by a capital programme for primaries. The aim is to spend £8.2 billion by 2011, with around 200 rebuilt or refurbished schools opening each year. But what of the existing schools? Good examples are comparable with other public amenities such as town halls, theatres and railway stations. Indeed, over 5,000 school buildings are listed for their special architectural and/or historic interest (Fig 1). Although not all were built as schools and many are now in other uses, this number includes large numbers of public and state school buildings that still serve their original purpose. Yet the two strands face very different prospects, with the public schools revered and preserved, though updated and extended, while the state schools are rebuilt. Have the latter any value, other than the sentimental? English Heritage's experience suggests they still have something to teach us.

Victorian schools have a visual interest as local landmarks, whether in a small rural settlement, or standing out above a sea of dense late 19th-century housing (*opposite*). This was most famously described by Sherlock Holmes to Dr Watson:

'Look at those big, isolated clumps of buildings rising up above the slates, like brick islands in a lead-coloured sea.'

'The board-schools.'

'Light-houses, my boy! Beacons of the future! Capsules with hundreds of bright little seeds in each, out of which will spring the wiser, better England of the future.' [1]

'Beacons of the future'. Holmes and Watson have their conversation on a train rattling through Clapham Junction. Looking up, they would have seen Lavender Hill School on Latchmere Road, of 1888–91 by T J Bailey, with its separate building for pupil teachers. The buildings were adapted as flats in 1993 by the Birmingham developers Sapcote, one of the first board schools to be converted in this way.
[AP26247/038]

Figure 1
Icknield Street School, Birmingham, 1883 by Martin and Chamberlain, one of the finest surviving board schools by this noted local firm, listed grade II* and in partial use as a Muslim centre.
[© Elain Harwood]

Research on schools is growing. More is now understood about the work of the School Boards founded in the 1870s, which pioneered new styles of architecture and classroom planning as elementary education offered something more than just reading, writing and arithmetic – colloquially known as the 'three Rs'. The quest to encourage the child by improving natural light and ventilation in its surroundings was further developed in the 20th century, particularly in the years 1907–14 and either side of the Second World War. Privately funded schools included some advancement in more modern facilities – for example, in nursery schools of lightweight construction or for the teaching of science – but many more were consciously historicist; though well-equipped, many were ill-planned.

England's post-war state schools received a relatively high level of funding compared with hospitals and other public buildings, and they were admired internationally – a Nottinghamshire County Council design won the highest award at the Milan Triennale (an international architectural exhibition) in 1960. Examples range from the austere, prefabricated primary schools of the late 1940s – in which every detail was carefully thought out from a child-size perspective – to the sturdy brick atria of Hampshire County Council's programme of the 1980s that still influences the design of schools today.

The challenge is to update the most architecturally interesting of these schools to give the best of both worlds, providing education to the highest

Figure 2 (right)
Infant School, Romney Avenue, Lockleaze, Bristol, by
Richard Sheppard, Robson and Partners, 1950. This and
the neighbouring junior school were the first schools
prefabricated of aluminium built as part of a special
programme by the Bristol Aeroplane Company, which
was looking to diversify after the war. The junior school
has been demolished but the infant school survives, much
refurbished.
[DP057764]

Figure 3
The Ragged School (Colwick Road Schools), Nottingham,
1859, restored as offices of the Nottinghamshire Wildlife
Trust after years of dereliction.
[© Elain Harwood]

modern standards within an environment that is itself a learning tool, encouraging a child's visual awareness, sense of community and place, and an appreciation of history. The loss of such buildings – with their large and bright classrooms – and the consequent effect on local distinctiveness, although impossible to quantify, should not be underestimated. It would be counterproductive if 'Building Schools for the Future' led to attractive and still functional buildings being swept away unnecessarily, especially given the world's declining material resources. English Heritage has produced a model brief showing local authorities how to determine the importance of the schools in their buildings portfolio and how to assign priorities for retention; there is also guidance on refurbishment, replacement and disposal (Figs 2 and 3). Additionally, English Heritage has worked closely with the Department for Children, Schools and Families and its forebears, and in 2005 published *The Future of Historic School Buildings* to demonstrate how the juxtaposition of new and old makes for exciting places as well as fit-for-purpose learning environments. This book reinforces that message, explaining the criteria a school must meet for its designation as a building of special architectural or historic interest, and offering a series of case study schools that have been successfully updated or given new uses. Its main aim, however, as with other titles in the Informed Conservation series, is that of explaining the importance of the buildings in question.

2

The earliest surviving schools

Until the 19th century most schools were built at the expense of private benefactors or entrepreneurs, with only modest investment by town and parish vestries. The result was a provision that was haphazard in both distribution and quality. The charitable schools of the Middle Ages often formed part of an endowment with almshouses, as at Ewelme, Oxfordshire, built in 1437.[2] Winchester and Eton Colleges, founded in 1382 and 1440 respectively, included education among a number of activities based around the running of a chapel and, at Eton, of almshouses for poor and disabled men. The schoolrooms were modest, with teaching delivered by rote and superintended by the older boys – a portent of early 19th-century practice. Other schools were built for young choristers at the cathedrals and larger churches – that at Canterbury first recorded in 1085–7 and today retaining one wall of the *nova scola noviciorum* under construction in 1397.

A wave of school building followed the Reformation. Protestant grammar schools such as the King's School at Canterbury, Kent, of 1541, were still religious foundations and many were built in or next to the churchyard, like the domestic-looking grammar school built at Walton near Liverpool by 1613. Some occupied conventual remains, but others were wholly new. By the late 16th century high, light schoolrooms were being built, with accommodation for a master and usher at one end, and a few also took in boarders. Most adopted a local vernacular style, exemplified by the tiny elementary school at Woolton, Liverpool, of *c* 1600 with vestigially Gothic arched windows (*opposite*). More elaborate is Peacock's School in Rye, Sussex, built in 1636 and early in its use of Dutch gables and giant pilasters (Fig 4). Many schools were founded by individual legacies, while others were supported by a town council or parish rates. More complex was Christ's Hospital, which opened in 1552 when Edward VI granted the City of London the Grey Friars' buildings on Newgate Street as a school and foundling hospital (Fig 5). Christ's Hospital's uniform of long coats and yellow stockings, its development of a commercial or English-based programme as well as a classical curriculum, and the teaching of poor orphans – girls as well as boys – provided a model for foundations around the country. School building peaked around 1620, but was revived after the Restoration as is testified by the number of surviving buildings, some still in school use.

Woolton Old School, School Lane, Woolton, Liverpool. A plaque gives the date 1610, but this may not be accurate. It is shown in a watercolour of 1947 by A H Jones. [Liverpool Record Office, Liverpool Libraries]

Figure 4
Peacock's School in Rye (Sussex), built in 1636 –
now a shop.
[© Elain Harwood]

Figure 5
Christ's Hospital, City of London. Founded in 1552, it was rebuilt after the Great Fire of London in consultation with Sir Christopher Wren. The writing school was added in 1696 to designs by Nicholas Hawksmoor. The building was demolished in 1902 when the school moved out to Horsham, Sussex.
[City of London, London Metropolitan Archives]

More elaborate buildings followed after 1660. Courteenhall School in Northamptonshire, of 1680, retains its large schoolroom lined with long desks for the boys on either side, and at one end is a pulpit-like desk for the master. Sir John Moore, partly responsible for the rebuilding of Christ's Hospital after the Great Fire of London, built a lavish school at Appleby Magna, Leicestershire, erected in 1693–7 at a cost of £2,800 (Fig 6). As at Christ's Hospital he solicited advice from Sir Christopher Wren, whose ideas were adapted by the local architect William Wilson as a three-storey building with a

large schoolroom containing a stepped area of seating, or gallery, facing the master's desk. The result is a rectangular block with a covered arcade between its two projecting wings, and its height and central cupola give it the appearance of a country house. Moore's school also demonstrated how, by increasing the number of fee-paying boarders, the masters of grammar schools could ensure their financial security, and marked a trend for accommodating them above the school room rather than in less carefully supervised lodgings in the village. Other schools evolved as a series of separate buildings, for example at Risley,

Figure 6
Appleby Magna School (Leics), erected in 1693–7. A design was commissioned from Sir Christopher Wren, but was modified by a local 'ingenious gentleman', William Wilson. His elevations are said to have met with Wren's approval.
[Mike Williams]

Figure 7
Latin House, Risley (Derbys), built in 1706 by Elizabeth
Grey. A school of 1593 was extended with this delightful
Baroque house for pupils, master and usher.
[© Elain Harwood]

Derbyshire, where the Latin House was built in 1706 by a wealthy heiress, Elizabeth Grey, just east of an earlier school founded in 1593 alongside the church (Fig 7). Mrs Grey endowed a further schoolhouse, partly for girls, in 1720, and in 1758 an identical English school for boys was built still further east. As the Latin House quickly devolved to the master and his private boarders, the Risley complex demonstrates the range of education available in the 18th century. Many children were educated in privately run academies, such as Powell's School in Cirencester, Gloucestershire, opened in 1740, and that run by

Mr and Mrs Holt in Walton, near Liverpool (Figs 8 and 9). It was from the post-Restoration years that Eton and Winchester began to attract large numbers of wealthy fee-paying boys in addition to charitable 'scholars'. In the 18th century Westminster similarly expanded, becoming second in size only to Eton, with a new dormitory built in 1722 to Lord Burlington's designs.

The beginning of the 18th century saw the building of more elementary schools, often in conjunction with poor relief, almshouses and other charitable bequests. The Blue Coat School was founded in Caxton Street, Westminster, by voluntary subscriptions in 1688 and moved to a specially-designed building in 1709. Many urban institutions boarded their pupils to ensure good discipline at all times. A product of this growth in elementary education was the separation of schooling for wealthy and poor children, and the emergence of schools giving girls a basic training in reading, sewing and knitting. These schools emphasised religion and moral welfare, while many at first combined education with some manual work to support the school (Fig 10). Outside London there were few such large charity schools, save Liverpool's Blue Coat School (Fig 11), founded in 1708 by sea captain Bryan Blundell, who provided

Figure 10
Newcomen's Charity Schools and St Saviour's Parochial School, Bowling Green Lane, Southwark, by G Yates, 1826.
[City of London, London Metropolitan Archives, Manning and Bray Collection]

Figure 11
Liverpool's Blue Coat School, now Bluecoat Chambers. The school was founded in 1708 by sea captain Bryan Blundell who paid for this imposing building in 1717–25. The architect is unknown. The building was saved from demolition by William Lever, the munificent soap manufacturer, when the school closed in 1906 and it has since been a college, library and art gallery. [DP045346]

Figure 12 (above)
Society of Friends' Boarding School at Ackworth, near
Wakefield (W Yorks), opened in 1779, from a photograph
of the 1890s.
[BB83/3178B]

Figure 13 (left)
The school today.
[Mike Williams]

new premises in 1717, again with facilities for boarders to distance them from their impoverished parents, who were seen as a bad influence. The Beneficial School for educating the poor boys of Portsmouth, Hampshire, was built in 1784 by a group of successful local tradesmen, with a large schoolroom on the ground floor for some thirty boys, and a room for its meetings above, a plan form that is still readable. An outstanding surviving example of a publicly-provided school dedicated to commercial subjects is the Corporation's Academy at Berwick-on-Tweed, Northumberland, set up in 1798 for boys and girls, and modelled on the progressive burgh schools of Scotland, with six classrooms devoted to different subjects.

During the 18th century a new impetus was given to education with the rise of new dissenting communities, who built schools to pass on their religious teaching. The Moravians set up schools soon after their arrival in England in 1738, at Fulneck in West Yorkshire (1753) and at Ockbrook, Derbyshire, where the school house dates from 1799. The most impressive non-conformist survival is the Society of Friends' Boarding School at Ackworth, near Wakefield, West Yorkshire, which in 1779 took over a Foundling Hospital to give poor children an elementary education according to the faith. The building, originally from 1758–65, has the scale of a country house but an institutional austerity that is denoted in its severe Tuscan order (Figs 12 and 13). More modest were the Sunday schools founded from the late 18th century, which taught the rudiments of reading and the scriptures for some four hours each Sunday. Most were small halls of little architectural pretension, erected close to, abutting or underneath a chapel.

In some early industrial centres massive Sunday schools were built, such as that in Roe Street, Macclesfield, Cheshire, founded by subscriptions in 1813. At four storeys high and ten windows wide it is as large as the silk mills on which the town's prosperity was based (Fig 14).

Figure 14
Roe Street Sunday School, Macclesfield (Ches), erected by voluntary subscriptions in 1813, and now in partial museum use. A school first opened here in 1796 and the memorial on the right commemorates its founder, John Whitaker.
[© Elain Harwood]

3

When money wins: the growth of public and charitable schools, 1800–1870

As provincial cities industrialised and expanded, more poor children were found wandering the streets, a pattern seen in London and the ports a century before. The 1802 Factory Act required mill owners to provide elementary instruction for its child workers, but a lack of inspectors meant the law was rarely enforced. A few benevolent industrialists set up schools, which are not only rare but so utilitarian as to be hard to identify today. More common were Dame schools, usually run by an elderly, barely literate woman who for a small fee taught reading and sewing. Ragged Schools offered basic literacy, with perhaps a little vocational training, a soup kitchen and adult classes. A national Ragged School Union was formed in 1844, and 32 schools were established in Liverpool alone by 1853. Such schools represent a larger and little known under-class of schools, supported by local philanthropists and churches, which provided a part-time education (Figs 15 and 16). As more children survived infancy and the Factory Acts became tougher, so demands for education grew.

More formal schooling offered the challenge of how to teach very large numbers cheaply. The solutions reflected a Benthamite concern for supervision and order, mainly based around a monitorial system in which older children took the younger ones through set lessons, usually individually, and through whom one master and mistress could control some three hundred children. Andrew Bell first wrote in 1797 of teaching using monitors in India, and his became known as the Madras system after it was fully published in 1807.[3] The schoolroom was arranged informally, and a detailed plan form was only evolved by his followers, in particular the National Society for Promoting the Education of the Poor in the Principles of the Established Church, founded in 1811. Its report of 1815 recommended setting desks and benches around the edge of a room, with movable benches (and work tables for girls' sewing) so that most of the teaching could be in small, flexible groups in the centre. Many classes were held standing up.

Joseph Lancaster offered a structured approach from the first, published in 1811 as *Hints and Directions for Building, Fitting up and Arranging School-Rooms on the British System of Education*. Desks were to be firmly fixed facing the master, and the sides of the room left clear for groups to work with their monitor and to study lesson boards hung on the walls. Where possible the desks were to be set on a rake, to give the master on a platform control over the children as a thespian might command a theatre. Lancaster's supporters formed

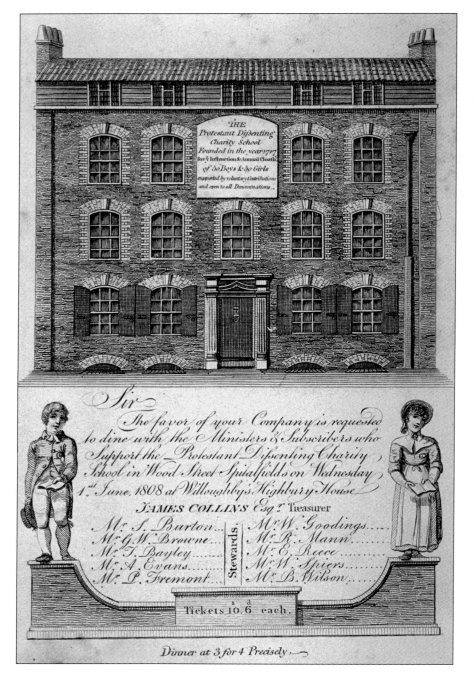

Figure 15
An invitation to a dinner for subscribers to the Protestant Dissenting Charity School in Wood Street, now Wilkins Street, Spitalfields, in 1808. Such dinners were important fund-raisers.
[City of London, London Metropolitan Archives]

Figure 16
Field Lane Ragged School, sometimes called West Street or
Chick Lane, Smithfield, by George Cruickshank, c 1850.
A typical picture of disorder.
[City of London, London Metropolitan Archives]

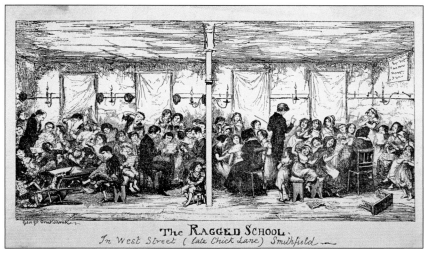

Figure 17
Wilderspin's infants' school moved, in 1830, to a new
building in St James's Square, Cheltenham (Glos) and
survives today as an office. This print dates from 1838.
[Gloucestershire Archives]

the Royal Lancasterian Association in 1810, from 1814 the British and Foreign School Society, which evolved his ideas after he left for America in 1818.

The monitorial system was first challenged by Samuel Wilderspin, a pioneer in specialist teaching for infants, for whom he established the first dedicated schools in the 1820s. He argued that infants needed more direct teaching from the master or mistress, and recommended building a small classroom off the main schoolroom for such group teaching. An infant school based on his ideas opened in 1828 in St James's Square, Cheltenham, Gloucestershire (Fig 17). Wilderspin thus evolved the 'simultaneous method' of teaching large numbers of children all at once, or what in the 20th century became known as 'chalk and talk'. He later introduced stepped seating or

Figure 18
The British School at Hitchin (Herts) is unique in retaining a five-step gallery for smaller children. This was added, in 1853, to a large classroom built in 1837 on Lancaster's monitorial system.
[F980083]

'galleries' into his schoolrooms so that large groups could be taught together – again an initiative begun with very small children and then disseminated to all ages. He was also among the first to encourage the provision of playgrounds with equipment for children to exercise on (p 16). David Stow expanded these ideas in a model school opened in Glasgow in 1826 and in a book, *The Training System*, published in 1836. His schoolroom had a gallery set behind an open area where groups of children could stand around a monitor, and a separate classroom. Meanwhile the National and British Societies, associated respectively with the Church of England and non-conformity, promoted plain new buildings, usually with a teacher's house to one side. The British School at Hitchin, Hertfordshire, founded in 1810, was rebuilt in 1837 on Lancaster's monitorial system, to which was added in 1853 a five-step gallery (Fig 18). Unusually, this survives and the school is now a museum (*see* Fig 93, p 94). At Barton-upon-Humber's National Schools, North Lincolnshire, built in 1844–5 by William Hey Dykes in collaboration with Wilderspin, the outline of the gallery survived as a guide to its restoration (Fig 19).[4]

In 1833 the government finally acceded to the benefits of educating its future workforce, and offered grants through the National and British Societies. With denominational differences at their height, the government made no attempt to dictate the curriculum, but it advised on the buildings – though here, too, the Societies initially retained an upper hand. However, from

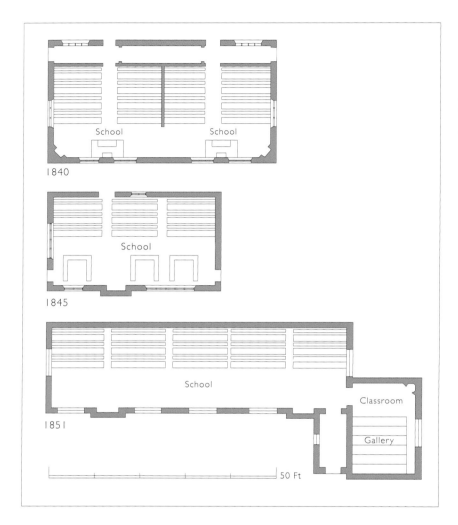

School

School

1840

School

1845

School

Classroom

1851

Gallery

50 Ft

Figure 20
Samples of plans prepared by the Education Committee,
1840, 1845 and 1851, showing the evolution of
classrooms and galleries.
[Redrawn from Seaborne 1971, 201]

1839 a government Education Committee took responsibility for approving building plans and appointed the first school inspectors. It recognised that more qualified teachers would be needed, and in 1846 the Committee's first Secretary, Sir James Kay-Shuttleworth, introduced a system from the Netherlands whereby pupil teachers aged between 14 and 17 were apprenticed to a master before going to a 'normal school' to qualify as an assistant teacher. In 1840 the Committee produced 16 ideal plans related to a 'mixed method' of monitored and simultaneous teaching, with desks on shallow steps preferred to Wilderspin's steep galleries (Fig 20).

Figure 21
Watercolour of the village
school at Aynhoe (Northants),
by Lili Cartwright, c *1845,*
showing gallery seating, forms,
lesson posts, blackboard, map-
stand, writing desks and many
improving texts.
[Private Collection/
The Bridgeman Art Library]

A schoolmaster's house was included in the designs, but became eligible for grants only in 1843. Less ambitious plans followed in 1845, followed in 1848 by proposals from the National Society that gave greater emphasis to the monitorial system. Classrooms were introduced only slowly, while the inexperience of pupil teachers and even of assistant teachers meant that the head had to maintain a degree of supervision. The 'class' was thus usually arranged as a block of desks in a larger room, separated by curtains and with a gallery where two classes could be taught at once (Fig 21). This system was set out in a memorandum by the Education Committee in 1851, and its features were adopted in schools into the 1880s.

Special provision was also made for workhouse children, to divert them from the traps of poverty or delinquency that had befallen their parents. Special boarding schools, sometimes known as 'barrack schools' and forerunners of the cottage homes promoted by Dr Barnardo, were built by larger workhouse unions to train these children for domestic service or a trade. The surviving fragments of these buildings can be impressive, including the centrepiece of the former Central London District School in Hanwell, Ealing, built in 1856 for a thousand children from the City of London and Southwark Union. A larger survival is the school at Stoke-on-Trent, Staffordshire (1866) – 21 bays long, with classrooms on the ground floor and dormitories above.

The 1830s saw Gothic and Tudor styles preferred to neo-Georgian models, thought appropriate to the religious enthusiasm behind so much education (Fig 22). That more schools were built by architects reflected an increasingly sophisticated patronage as well as the emergence of a specialised profession aided by model plans. A few adopted the austere Gothic style of Commissioners' churches, notably the Clerkenwell Parochial School in London, of 1838 by William Chadwell Milne (Fig 23). More schools adopted a stripped Tudor style for its economy, and for its associations with the great educational

Figure 22 (above, left)
St John's Church School, Worksop (Notts),
built in 1873 (demolished).
[Nottinghamshire Archives, CC/ED/11/4 /124]

Figure 23 (above, right)
Clerkenwell Parochial School in London, of 1838
by William Chadwell Milne. A good example of the
stripped Gothic style popular for church schools in
the early 19th century.
[© Elain Harwood]

Figure 24
Boys' Grammar School, Wakefield (W Yorks),
now part of the Queen Elizabeth Grammar School,
1833–4 by Richard Lane, an early example of a school
in the Gothic style.
[Mike Williams]

drive of the Reformation. The Boys' Grammar School in Wakefield, West Yorkshire, by Richard Lane, from 1833–4, uses a Perpendicular Gothic, with leaded lights (Fig 24). More elaborate Gothic Revival schools were built for wealthy landowners to blend into the contrived idyll of their estate villages. One of the finest was designed by A W N Pugin as the Roman Catholic Parish School at Spetchley, Worcestershire, in 1841 (Fig 25). It was a forerunner of many Gothic village schools, some designed by church specialists like William

Butterfield and George Edmund Street. Other schools were more romantically picturesque, including the village school at Somerleyton, Suffolk, built by John Thomas in 1845 as part of an estate layout (Fig 26). New schools also made an architectural ensemble with a church and vicarage as the centre of a new industrial settlement, notably in such model towns as Saltaire, West Yorkshire, founded by Sir Titus Salt in 1851, but equally in less homogeneous mining and railway settlements – such as Swindon, Wiltshire, and in the new suburbs of major cities.

The churches also began to build substantial schools for middle-class children, offering a broad education suited to a commercial career. The flight of Catholic schools from Europe during the Revolutionary and Napoleonic wars led to the foundation of Stonyhurst in Lancashire by the Jesuits in 1794, followed by schools at Ampleforth, North Yorkshire, in 1802 (Fig 27) and Downside near Bath, Somerset, in 1814. Stonyhurst was extended in 1808–10 with schoolrooms and dormitories, and also an 'academy room' for teaching science. Middle-class provision for dissenters included the Quaker School at Bootham, York, and the Wesleyan Proprietary Grammar School, Sheffield (Fig 28), designed in 1837 by

Figure 25 (above)
The Roman Catholic Parish School at Spetchley (Worcs), by A W N Pugin, 1841. It shows the simplicity of his Gothic architecture.
[Mike Williams]

Figure 26 (left)
A village school at Somerleyton (Suffolk), of 1845 by John Thomas, showing how picturesque an estate school could be.
[© Elain Harwood]

Figure 27 (opposite)
Ampleforth School (N Yorks), founded in 1802. Buildings of many dates and styles are huddled round the abbey church of 1922–61 by Sir Giles Scott, and the main school building of 1861 by Charles Hansom with its prominent gables. The earliest buildings lie behind the trees to the north (right), while later buildings to the south include the theatre-cum-gymnasium of 1911–14, denoted by a fleche. Boarding houses are set around the perimeter.
[AP20838/036]

William Flockton in a Greek Revival style seen as embodying enlightenment – unlike the 'superstitious' Gothic. More ambitious still was the Protestant Dissenters' Grammar School, Mill Hill, Barnet, a proprietary school run by its shareholders, built in 1825–7 to the designs of Sir William Tite with individual classrooms for teaching modern subjects such as mathematics and French. Rugby School was rebuilt in 1809–16 by Henry Hakewill, with separate rooms

Figure 28
Wesleyan Proprietary Grammar School, now King Edward VII Upper School, Sheffield, 1837–8 by William Flockton, listed grade II* and still in school use. [Mike Williams]

for each form, so that classes could be taught orally, and with studies for the boys (*see* inside back cover). King Edward's School in Birmingham was rebuilt in 1838 by Charles Barry and A W N Pugin, with two large schoolrooms, one for classical subjects and the other (the 'Library') for modern subjects. A large complex in Bedford by Edward Blore, opened in 1834, included a commercial school, boys' and girls' elementary schools and a hospital school, all supported by the local Harper Trust. There were also many private schools for middle-class boys and girls, operated from converted accommodation and generally short-lived (Fig 29).

More public schools were refounded and rebuilt from the mid-19th century onwards. Dulwich College, London, founded in 1605, received a windfall of £100,000 in compensation for three railway lines cut through its estate. This prompted an investigation by the Charity Commissioners, leading in 1857 to the reconstitution of the college and in 1866–70 to a new day school by Charles Barry Junior (Fig 30). Lancing College, Sussex, was the first of a

Figure 29 (above)
Clarendon Academy, Bradford, dated 1867. A rare surviving example of a modest yet successful private school from the 19th century.
[© Elain Harwood]

Figure 30 (right)
Dulwich College, London, rebuilt by Charles Barry Junior in 1866–70 to give the school a new image after its reconstitution and demonstrating its new-found wealth and popularity.
[DD97/00139]

Figure 31
An aerial view of Lancing College (Sussex), founded in
1848 by Nathaniel Woodard. The first of a group of 20
schools for the middle classes, Lancing was intended for
the sons of 'clergymen and other gentlemen', and its first
buildings were by the ecclesiastical architect R C
Carpenter. The dramatic chapel that dominates the
skyline was begun by his son R H Carpenter in 1868
but never completed, and the west front was added
in the 1960s by Stephen Dykes Bower.
[AP26234 1010]

series of strongly Anglican foundations by Nathaniel Woodard that established
a pattern of middle-class education. Begun to the designs of R C Carpenter in
1848, and developed by his son R H Carpenter after 1855, its highlight is a
soaring chapel set high on the South Downs (Fig 31). On a smaller scale,
Nottingham High School of 1513 was re-founded as a fee-paying school in
1855 and in 1868 moved to a more salubrious site on the edge of the city,
where a baronial Gothic building was designed by Thomas Simpson with large
schoolrooms for classical and modern subjects (Fig 32). While schools in the
large towns evolved as day schools, those in more rural locations developed as
boarding schools, including that at Malvern, built in 1863–5 by Charles
F Hansom. The Girls' Public Day School Trust was founded in 1872 to provide
fee-paying schools for girls. Most of its premises were converted houses but,
where it could afford to commission new buildings, its architects – usually
local men until the Trust appointed its own architect, James Osborne Smith,
in 1897 – followed the model of the boys' schools with classrooms set round
a central hall, reflecting the low importance afforded traditional domestic
subjects by the Trust.

The dispersal of public schools to suburban and even rural locations
continued into the 20th century. Charterhouse left London for Godalming,
Surrey, in 1872, where buildings were provided by P C Hardwick in a Gothic
style, and Christ's Hospital moved to Horsham, West Sussex, in 1894. There,
Aston Webb and Ingress Bell used a Tudor style based on, they claimed, 'the
traditional type of our university towns', but set out in blocks rather than
quadrangles as more sanitary. The north front of Big School incorporates late
17th-century statuary and ornament, some by Grinling Gibbons, in a Wrennish
composition.[5] The pressure on public schools to develop science teaching was
greatest in industrial towns, though even here traditional styles continued to be
used, as at Wolverhampton Grammar School in 1874 and Bablake School in
Coventry, extended in 1890. Only the most specialist science schools, such as
the evangelist John Rutherford established in Newcastle in 1877 for all classes
and both sexes, adopted a more functional idiom.

4

The school boards, 1870–1902

The years after 1870 saw the greatest change in British education, when the state began to replace the churches as the principal source of elementary schooling. From 1880 education became compulsory until the age of 10 or a certain standard was reached, whichever was the later. The minimum age was raised to 11 in 1893 and to 12 in 1899. The resulting basic literacy is reflected in the advance of more skilled, scientific trades and in the growth of the popular press. By 1902 steps were also being taken by the larger boards to provide vocational training, swimming lessons and more advanced teaching for the brighter children.

These changes began with the 1870 Education Act, promoted by W E Forster, MP for Bradford, to fill the gaps in the voluntary system 'at least cost in public money'.[6] The Act first encouraged the churches to build schools, with special building grants. But where such efforts were inadequate, it allowed for school boards, comprising up to 15 members elected by the ratepayers (Fig 33). Most boards were split along religious and political lines. Women were entitled to vote and to stand as candidates from 1870, when four were elected, the first in any British elected authorities (Fig 34).

Boards in the countryside were very small, as they covered a single parish; only very occasionally were they permitted to form unions (Fig 35). In urban areas, where the voluntary system was most deficient, they covered the whole town or city concerned. There was thus a great contrast between a tiny parish like Awsworth, Nottinghamshire, which in 1877 elected a board of four shopkeepers and a miner to buy land from the local colliery and initially erect a single school (Fig 36), and city boards building for thousands of children. The Education Department, while maintaining common standards of space and construction across the country, were cautious in promoting changes to the curriculum and general layouts, and it was the city school boards that introduced new ideas in these areas.

The Act inspired the Anglican, Roman Catholic and Methodist churches to redouble their efforts to provide schools rather than see education pass to a board, where religious teaching had to be non-denominational. Other non-conformists supported the board schools. The Education Department's inspectors, now backing their more rigorous standards with small grants, ensured the new church schools were rather more spacious and better lit than their predecessors, though without support from the rates most were built to

Figure 33 (above)
Former offices to the Bootle School Board, 1888
by Thomas Cox, now disused.
[DP059528]

(opposite)
Summerfield School, Birmingham, 1885 by Martin
and Chamberlain, now a community centre.
[Mike Williams]

Figure 34
The first London School Board, elected in 1870, attending a meeting. Women could vote in school board elections, and could stand as members. Elizabeth Garrett was elected for Marylebone in 1870 with 47,000 votes, and Emily Davies was returned for Greenwich. Outside London, Flora Stevenson was elected in Edinburgh and Lydia Becker in Manchester, and a few more women stood in later elections. John Whitehead Wallow, c 1870. [Guildhall Art Gallery, City of London]

tighter budgets than the board schools. Churches, however, found difficulty in raising funds to maintain their schools once built, especially after the abolition of basic fees in 1891 gave board schools a clear advantage. Having campaigned volubly against a board, the High Church vicar of Sneinton, Nottingham, Canon Vernon Hutton, in 1875 had to accept one imposed by the Education Department because his church school could not cope with a rapidly expanding population. Hutton's obstinacy contrasts with the Nottingham Board, where the Anglican and non-conformist lobbies were led by education reformers who worked together with rare harmony, and Leicester, where the first chairman was the Liberal churchman and educationalist Canon David Vaughan.

In Bradford, West Yorkshire, the first board was selected by the mayor to avoid the aggravation and expense of an election; thereafter Liberals were in the majority.

Board schools have many common features: most are simple buildings in brick or occasionally stone, with large windows and – usually – rows of gables. All had to meet the strictures of the Education Department, who had to approve the site, plans and costs before agreeing a loan. Yet there was no standard design. The earliest schools show a bewildering variety of styles, until gradual specialisation by particular firms and the publication of their designs

Figure 35
Fairfields Primary School, Basingstoke (Hants), 1887–8 by Charles Bell. A confident-looking school for what was then a small town, but it is only one room deep. It overlooks the cricket ground and a plaque commemorates John Arlott, a pupil here.
[© Elain Harwood]

led to a greater homogeneity in elevations and plan types. Their designs combined economy with a concern for good light that produced high roofs and large gables, and a sense of local pride reflected in the buildings' emblematic signage and many plaques. The scale of the schools, whether in a city or small village, made them enduring local landmarks – the 'beacons' proclaimed by Sherlock Holmes as his train hurtled through Clapham Junction Station are still prominent on the hillside towards Battersea Rise (pp viii and 1).

Only a partial picture can be derived from surviving structures: almost all the earliest Sheffield schools survive (Fig 37), while none of the 10 built in Manchester before 1880 exists today. Some boards, like Sheffield and Leeds, took on a salaried architect, while others, including Manchester and Nottingham, held competitions for each building. Contestants who thus gained proficiency in school design solicited work from smaller neighbouring boards. Nottingham architect R C Sutton failed to secure work in Nottingham, but his expertise was found adequate by nearby Greasley and Awsworth Boards; after A N Bromley became consultant architect to the Nottingham Board in 1890 he secured a commission to build a school at Beeston, realised in 1896–7. Some architects became schools specialists, including Brightwen Binyon who built six schools in Ipswich and four in Swindon. Young architects gained experience in public building through designing schools, as Ernest George found working for Harrow School Board, where he was appointed in 1874.

The Queen Anne style

The School Board for London was the first to be founded under the 1870 Act and was the most influential. In July 1871 E R Robson was appointed its first architect. Initially, schools were designed by private architects under his supervision, mainly through limited competitions, but after the first opened in 1873 Robson gained direct control of design and began to produce standardised buildings more quickly. He had recently formed a partnership with J J Stevenson, a pioneer of the Queen Anne style, which adopted the sash windows and red brick vernacular idiom of many houses found in southern England from the late 17th and early 18th centuries. This lent itself to the repetitive, large-scale design required for schools, and to the need for big

Figure 36
Awsworth School (Notts), 1877–8 by R C Sutton. Now a private house.
[© Elain Harwood]

Figure 37
Heeley Board School, Gleadless Road, Sheffield, of 1890, and extended in 1897, by C J Innocent. It was closed in 2006, following the opening of a new school alongside. A listed building, it was identified by SAVE Britain's Heritage as a Building at Risk in 2009.
[© Elain Harwood]

windows to light classrooms and halls. Above all, it offered a cheap, secular alternative to the Gothic style adopted by the denominational schools. It has long been assumed that Stevenson's was the formative influence, but the first schools in the style were by the private architects, notably Basil Champneys, whose Harwood Road School, Fulham (1873, demolished) was extensively published. The earliest surviving example is Seebright School, Hackney, by Charles Mileham from 1873. Robson's work from this period could be vestigially Gothic, as at Eagle Court School, Islington (1872–3), although in June 1872 he told the Architectural Association that 'a school should appear like a school, and not like a monastery, a town hall, or a set of almshouses'.[7] He and Stevenson exhibited Queen Anne designs at the Royal Academy in 1873 which gained them wide publicity. Their first surviving Queen Anne style

Figure 38
Bowling Green Lane School, Islington, 1873–5 by
E R Robson. One of his first schools in the Queen Anne
style – now partly occupied by Zaha Hadid Architects.
[© Elain Harwood]

Figure 39
Jonson Street School, Stepney, by T Roger Smith for the
London School Board, 1872–3 (demolished). It pioneered
the use of a separate hall and classrooms. Here, those for
infants, girls and boys are stacked one above the other.
[BL01028]

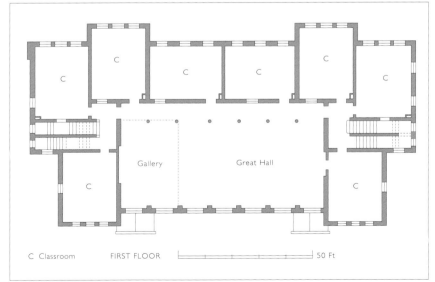

Figure 40
The influential plan by T Roger Smith for Jonson Street
School, Stepney.
[Based on Robson 1874 (1972), 304]

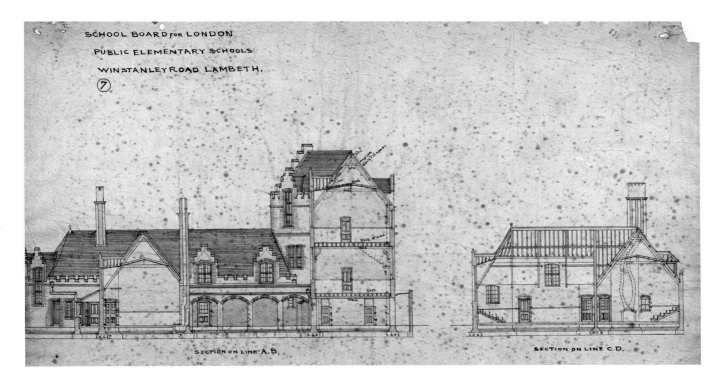

SCHOOL BOARD FOR LONDON
PUBLIC ELEMENTARY SCHOOLS
WINSTANLEY ROAD LAMBETH.

SECTION ON LINE A.B.

SECTION ON LINE C.D.

Figure 41
Winstanley Road Board School, Lambeth by Robson and Stevenson for the London School Board. It shows that as late as 1873 they were working in the Gothic style. Note the arcaded covered playground in the main block, and the gallery in the single-storey infants' wing, right.
[City of London, London Metropolitan Archives]

schools are Southwark Park School, Southwark (1873–4), with spandrel relief panels depicting children learning, and the former Bowling Green Lane School, Islington, of 1873–5 (Fig 38).

Initially, most board schools followed the schoolroom plan, usually with separate rooms for boys, girls and infants. Most had a gallery, and subsidiary classrooms – usually at either end of the schoolroom for best ventilation – where pupil teachers or young assistants taught under the supervision of the master or mistress. The schoolroom could not be superseded while there was a lack of qualified teachers. The London Board was the first to experiment with separate classrooms, for up to 80 children each, with a central schoolroom or hall based on German models, a requirement of its competition for Jonson Street School, Stepney, won by T Roger Smith in 1872 (Figs 39 and 40). Considered expensive, the experiment was not much repeated before 1880,

Figure 42 (left)
Ropery Street, Tower Hamlets. The school in
the foreground dates from 1874, by E R Robson,
and contrasts with the larger one to the rear by
T J Bailey of 1904.
[© Elain Harwood]

Figure 43 (opposite)
Catherine Street School, Hackney, a classic triple-decker
London board school with a rooftop playground,
photographed in 1887.
[BL06934]

when a hall became a formal requirement in London, and was widely adopted by other urban boards. Other features also became standard, particularly the triple-decker plan of a ground-floor infant school and covered play area, with separate schools for older girls on the first floor and boys on the second, each entered via their own lobbies and staircases. Some schools placed the infants in a single-storey wing, as seen in Robson and Stevenson's Winstanley Road School, Lambeth, designed in 1873 (Fig 41). After 1876 Robson's schools became larger and more mechanical in design, as he and his assistant T J Bailey organised their office on to a production-line footing. Succeeding Robson in 1883, Bailey evolved a bold and monumental massing which could be highly decorative (Fig 42). Where possible he placed the halls one above the other on the street frontage as the centrepiece of a soaring Baroque composition with symmetrical wings, turrets and finials, though as his larger schools were often designed to be built in stages many remained unfinished. London's most eye-catching board schools date from the Bailey era (Fig 43).

The Queen Anne style and central hall plan – sometimes called the Prussian model – spread across England. Robson himself took the style north when he was commissioned to design two schools in Sheffield, both completed

in 1880. His influence can be seen on schools by Innocent and Brown for the Sheffield Board, including Huntmans Gardens School where the classrooms were set around a semi-circular hall so they could be easily supervised by the head teacher. The Sheffield Board appointed the local architect C J Innocent in 1871 as a part-time member of staff, which ensured that the programme for its first 15 schools was handled professionally in every detail. Subsequently the board held competitions, often won by Innocent until his ideas were superseded by those of younger architects, notably W J Hale and A F Watson of Holmes and Watson.

Bradford rapidly gained a reputation for building generous and architecturally elaborate schools, built by five leading local firms (Fig 44). Education and child welfare were encouraged there from the mid-19th century after a series of riots prompted the industrialist Titus Salt to lead an investigation into the moral condition of the population. A flurry of church building followed, and the 1870 Act provided the means to follow suit with schools. Its first eight schools, completed in 1874, alarmed the Education Department by their expense, for Bradford had borrowed more from the Public Works Loan Board than any other board outside London, its debt more than twice that of Leeds. The designs were based on church architecture, most having an imposing bell tower and rose windows, with inside a lofty but often narrow schoolroom. Later schools, such as Great Horton School of 1886 by W J Morley, adopted a rich Queen Anne style copied by other boards in the area.

The Leeds School Board built 61 schools, using a variety of architects and styles. Richard Adams was appointed architect in 1873 and produced 35 red-brick schools, both Italianate and Gothic in style, including the Italianate Armley School of 1878. Other schools were designed by George Corson, along with the elaborate offices built alongside the Municipal Buildings in 1881. The Birmingham School Board employed Martin and Chamberlain between 1870 and 1901, and their 47 designs have a strong familial resemblance (p 32). J H Chamberlain (no relation to the local politician Joseph Chamberlain) believed that school architecture should offer children some compensation for their drab homes, and the schools are lively exercises in Ruskinian Gothic, with tile and terracotta decoration, well seen at Icknield Street School, opened in 1883. The style was developed further by William and Frederick Martin after Chamberlain's death that year, with ranges of gables clustered round a central

Figure 44
Lilycroft School, Bradford (W Yorks), one of the first board schools built there, in 1872–3, designed by Hope and Jardine in a lavish Gothic style.
[Mike Williams]

Figure 45
Fosse School, Leicester, of 1898, is one of Edward Burgess's most powerful designs, dominated by its plenum tower.
[© Elain Harwood]

lantern. Two- and occasionally three-storey schools were adopted because sites were small. The *Pall Mall Gazette* wrote in 1894 that, 'In Birmingham you may generally recognize a board-school by its being the best building in the neighbourhood. ... With lofty towers – which serve the utilitarian purpose also of giving excellent ventilation – gabled windows, warm red bricks, and stained glass, the best of the Birmingham board-schools have quite an artistic finish'.[8]

Most impressive was Martin and Chamberlain's concern for heating and ventilation, after 1890 adopting 'plenum' or forced air systems which are recognisable by towers and ventilation hoods that kept a supply of fresh air in constant circulation. Similar systems were used in Bradford, West Yorkshire, and Hanley, Staffordshire, and by Edward Burgess in Leicester, but they were an expensive alternative to pipes and radiators. A fine example by Burgess from 1898 is the Fosse School, now a neighbourhood centre and library (Fig 45).

By contrast Manchester placed a great emphasis on economy and its schools were austere. Competitions were held between local firms, several of whom became specialists in school building, including Royle and Bennett, Henry Lord, and Potts, Son and Hennings. The Manchester Board built 39 schools before 1902, all distinguished by large memorial stones with serial numbers, a practice continued by the local authority until 1913. Most had a central schoolroom rather than a specialised hall and a gaunt Gothic was common until the 1890s when a simple Renaissance style took over. But some were impressive in scale, notably Varna Street School, Openshaw, of 1896–7 for over 2000 children. Parishes within the city – Crumpsall, Levenshulme and Moss Side – built their own schools, as did Withington Urban District Council, although the school for the Moss Side Board (Fig 46), built in 1896 based on designs by Woodhouse and Willoughby, varied little from those of the Manchester Board itself. Elsewhere, a particularly fine Queen Anne design is Walter Brierley's masterpiece, the Scarcroft Road School in York, built in 1896 (Fig 47).

Schools were solidly constructed, yet spartan. Glazed brick and tiled surfaces made for easy cleaning and fumigation, with a few cupboards. Fitted desks gradually replaced galleries. Curtains separated early classrooms, until in the 1890s they were slowly superseded by glazed wooden partitions that could be folded back as required. Arched 'play sheds' on the ground floor, where children could exercise in bad weather, were most common on hilly

Figure 46 (left)
Manchester's schools matched London's in scale and were still more austere. Among the more elaborate is Moss Side Board School, though, as built in 1896, it differs slightly from the designs by architects Woodhouse and Willoughby. It is now an adult education centre.
[© Elain Harwood]

Figure 47 (below)
York has some fine board schools by the leading local architect Walter Brierley, of which the best is perhaps Scarcroft School, from 1896.
[Mike Williams]

(generally northern) sites, and in the earliest London schools such as Farncombe Street, Southwark (1874). In densely populated areas resort was made to rooftop playgrounds, notably in London's East End where the former Durward Street School, Whitechapel, of 1876–7, has the earliest-known example (Fig 48). Elsewhere covered play areas could be free-standing or abutting a wall.

Special schools

The larger school boards built special schools for disabled or disturbed children. London began classes for the deaf in 1874, followed later that year by ones for the blind. 'Industrial' schools provided manual and vocational training in the hope that even the most unruly youngsters could become self-respecting members of society. Most authorities passed these difficult children off to schools provided by the churches or the Poor Law, but the larger ones built their own, usually in the most austere of styles (Figs 49 and 50). In Leeds, William Landless built Czar Street industrial school (demolished) and added to existing school sites for blind, deaf and dumb children. In 1890 the London School Board resolved to provide special schools for children with learning difficulties, and built 24 between 1892 and 1896, usually as single-storey annexes in the grounds of large board schools, as at Hugh Myddelton, Islington, opened in 1896. In Sheffield A F Watson designed special schools for handicapped children at Newhall, opened in 1906, and Highfield in 1907. More commonly, by the 1890s many boards were adding specialist blocks, for the teaching of cookery or technical trades – sometimes as a shared resource

Figure 49 (below, left)
Shadwell Industrial School, Leeds, first opened as Edgar Street School in 1862. It became an approved school in 1933.
[Mike Williams].

Figure 50 (below)
The former Day Industrial School for Girls and Boys, Windmill Hills, Gateshead, designed by Thomas Oliver in 1878 and opened in 1880. The lower part to the left was the infant school.
[DP059483]

between several schools – and even swimming pools. In Bradford, Wapping Road School, originally built in 1877, was the first to add baths and a swimming pool, in 1897, while Usher Street was the first to provide school medicals for children, in 1899.

Higher grade schools

The board schools rapidly progressed beyond the teaching of elementary reading, writing and arithmetic. Leicester reported a curriculum that included history, geography, science, drawing, singing and drill, all of which earned grants from the Education Department after 1871. Cookery began in 1877 and music in 1878. But the bright child from a poor home still had little chance of gaining sufficient education to meet the rising demand for office workers and teachers. Leicester did not develop an advanced programme as the local public schools provided scholarships, although it ran extensive evening classes for adults. But for other progressive boards – notably Bradford, Sheffield, Nottingham, Halifax, Manchester, Leeds, Birmingham and London – a higher grade school was the height of their achievement. The Department of Science and Art, supporting vocational training since 1853, provided grants towards these schools. In Bradford, Feversham Street School, a Gothic design by Lockwood and Mawson from 1873, became a higher elementary school in 1876 partly at the suggestion of the Education Department's inspector, because the school could not attract sufficient elementary children (Fig 51). Purpose-built higher schools were usually located centrally – so that they could serve a wide area – and were large, with smaller classrooms and more specialist facilities. In Sheffield a central 'higher' school was built in 1876–80 as a stepping stone to Firth College – the future Sheffield University – in a complex by local architect T J Flockton with E R Robson. The long-standing Liberal chairman of the Birmingham School Board, George Dixon, personally funded a boys' technical school, The Bridge, from 1884 until it was superseded by a higher board school in 1892. Nottingham held a competition in 1896 for a flagship higher school with classes of only 40 children, won by R C Clarke. Manchester's Central Higher Grade School in Whitworth Street, now Sheena Simon College, designed by Potts, Son and Hennings and built between 1897 and 1901,

Figure 51 (above, left)
Feversham Street School, Bradford (W Yorks), was built by Lockwood and Mawson in 1873 in the wrong place – there were few children living nearby, so the building was remodelled as England's first higher elementary board school in 1876.
[Mike Williams]

Figure 52 (above)
Manchester's board schools were among the plainest in England. More decoration was allowed at the Central Higher Grade School in Whitworth Street (now Sheena Simon College), designed by Potts, Son and Hennings and built between 1897 and 1901.
[Mike Williams]

included 2 halls (for boys and girls), a manual instruction room, gymnasium, book room, typewriting room, machine room, library, art room, chemical and physical laboratories, and 2 lecture rooms, plus 4 classrooms for girls and 11 for boys (Fig 52). Still larger was the Central Higher Grade School, Leeds, built by Birchall and Kelly in 1889 and soon raised by William Landless, who added the rooftop playground. Next door stands the former Pupil Teacher College of 1900 by Walter Braithwaite (Fig 53); following the example of Liverpool in 1883 the larger boards built their own teacher training centres rather than relying on those of the churches.

Local authorities (mainly county councils) took an interest in higher education from the 1890s, when they were allowed to levy rates towards providing technical training, to which was added money previously given to the brewers on surrender of public house licences. Many built higher education colleges, polytechnics and 'monotechnics' related to single specific trades. Most of these ran daytime classes for children aged 13–15 – so-called 'junior techs' – while adult education was concentrated in evening classes. Terracotta was a popular material, seen at the Birkenhead Technical School, Cheshire, of 1900–2 by

Figure 53
The Pupil Teacher College in Leeds is particularly
handsome and prominent, built in 1900 by W S
Braithwaite, who was the last and perhaps finest of the
city's school board architects. It conveniently adjoins the
earlier Higher Grade School (1889 by Birchall and Kelly).
[Mike Williams]

William and Segar Owen, resplendently decorated with relief panels of eminent scientists. Other schools have plaques proclaiming their origins – the modest scale of the Bideford Technical School, Devon, of 1896, by G Malam Wilson, is belied by the size of the municipal plaque (*see* back cover). In 1898 the Technical Education Board of the London County Council (LCC) applied to take over the teaching of science and art in higher schools, which led in 1901 to a ruling in the House of Lords – the Cockerton judgment – that boards were acting illegally in providing adult education. This was used by the Conservative government as an excuse to transfer education from the largely Liberal boards to local authorities. Yet already an Act of 1899 had brought together the Education Department and the Department of Science and Art into a new Board of Education, heralding the unification of schooling at local level. In 1902 an Education Act abolished the 2,568 school boards in favour of the county and county borough councils, who were also given responsibility for the voluntary denominational schools. London's education passed to the LCC in 1903.

5

Local authorities take command, 1902–1918

The reorganisation of 1902 brought money to the voluntary school sector run by the churches, since local authorities were permitted to offer some funding towards building work. Rural areas also benefited, as for the first time there was a chance of secondary education. But many cities found that their councils were more parsimonious than the boards, with education treated as one responsibility among many. The building of elementary schools declined, albeit largely due to a falling birth rate, which meant that new schools were concentrated in developing suburbs and areas of expanding industry. Only in London and the larger cities facing land shortages did the tradition of multi-storey schools continue. Some schools could be elaborate examples of the Arts and Crafts style, such as Air Balloon Hill School, St George's, Bristol, of 1905 by LaTrobe and Watson (Fig 54), and the Kettlebridge School, Ouseburn, Sheffield, of 1904 by W J Hale.

As the government's policy of payment by results gave way to more general grants, so there was more scope for new ideas in education. Authorities slowly began to consider elementary school design from the point of view of the child as well as the teacher, while the open suburban sites encouraged the building of single-storey schools that maximised natural light and ventilation. Felix Clay

(opposite)
Ilkeston School (former Grammar School), 1911–14 by George Widdows for Derbyshire County Council.
[Mike Williams]

Figure 54 (right)
Air Balloon Hill School, St George's, Bristol, of 1905. The planning resembles that of earlier board schools but is one of the finest works by LaTrobe and Watson in their distinctive Arts and Crafts style.
[Mike Williams]

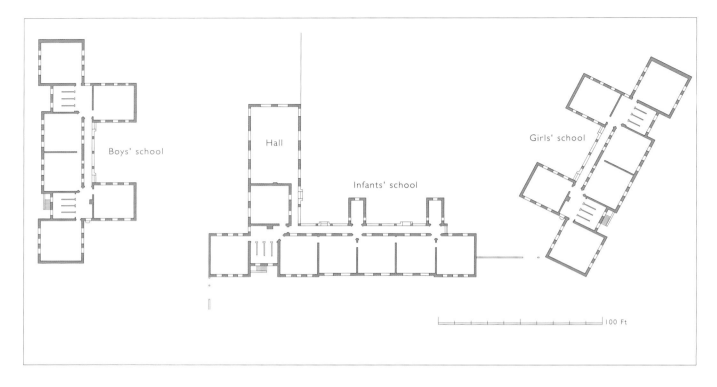

Boys' school

Hall

Infants' school

Girls' school

100 Ft

– longtime architect to the Board of Education – was later to write of the years 1907–14 as seeing a radical shift in school planning, remarking that it was one easily taken for granted so quickly did it become the norm in the 1920s. The first major conference on school hygiene was held in 1904, but the turning point came in 1907 when legislation by the Board of Health meant that schools became subject to regular medical inspections. Staffordshire's medical officer, George Reid, advocated that school design should be based around the needs of good health, in a report entitled 'The Planning of Schools with Reference to their Ventilation'. For Dorsett Road School in Darlaston, Reid and the County Architect, John Hutchings, devised a plan of three pavilions – for boys, girls and infants – with all the classrooms entered from an open verandah and with cross ventilation (Fig 55). Opened in 1907, it marked the death knell of central halls and was deemed so successful in reducing coughs and colds that the plan was widely adopted, both in Staffordshire and beyond.

These ideas were taken further by George Widdows, architect to Derbyshire County Council Education Committee from 1904 and County Architect from 1910 to 1936. Derbyshire's population increased in the 1890s

Figure 55
Plan of Dorsett Road Elementary School, Darlaston (Staffs) by John Hutchings, 1907 (demolished). [Redrawn from Seabourne and Lowe 1977, 83, and with permission from Staffordshire Record Office]

Figure 56
Highfield Primary School, Long Eaton. George Widdows's schools for Derbyshire County Council become more elaborate around 1911, and this is perhaps the most interesting of those planned, with broad marching corridors for indoor recreation.
[DP084971]

faster than that of any other county, thanks to the development of its coalfield and textile industries, leading Widdows to design or extend 60 elementary and 17 secondary schools. One of his most innovative schools, with cross ventilation and a 'marching corridor' for exercise, is Highfield Primary School, Long Eaton, built in 1911 in a neo-vernacular style (Fig 56). Elsewhere he commonly arranged his infant schools as a simple line of six classrooms, all with large south-facing windows. Classrooms for 60 children are set at either end with, between them, smaller rooms fronted by a covered verandah that provides access; above are dormer windows to give cross ventilation and natural light on both sides – though Widdows used electric light where available, most of his schools had originally to be lit by gas. The boys' and girls' classrooms were separated by cloakrooms and access to an assembly hall that was almost free-standing. Typical are Breaston Firfield from 1911, and Tibshelf

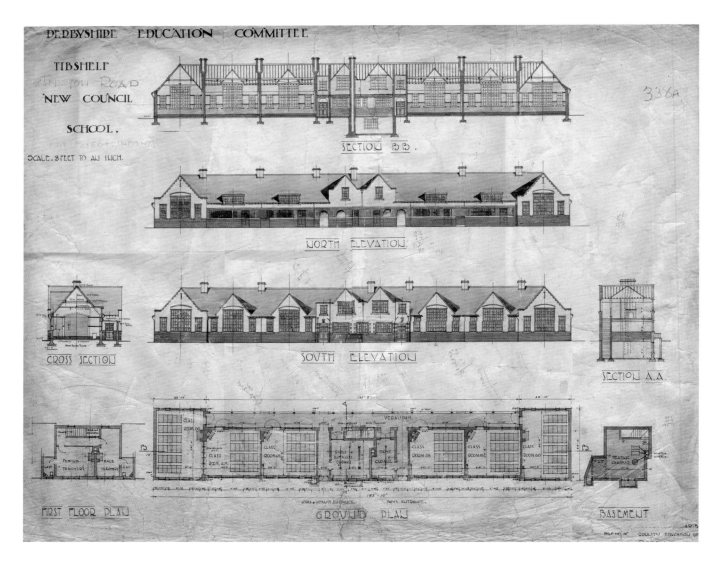

Figure 57
Tibshelf Townend Junior School, 1913–14, by George Widdows for Derbyshire Education Committee. This shows a typical range of six classrooms, the larger ones at either end, with the others linked by a verandah. Gables above this ensure the classrooms are lit from both sides. [Derbyshire County Council, Derbyshire Record Office, D2200/36/9. Reproduced by permission]

Townend (Fig 57) and North Wingfield Infants School from 1914. Schools in Alfreton (1907), South Normanton (1911) and Wirksworth (1912) have a central hall with classrooms set at each corner. In larger schools, such as at Ripley (1914) and Staveley (1926), Widdows set these lines of classrooms and verandahs around a series of courtyards (Figs 58–61). *The Builder* enthused in 1913 about 'the great work which Mr Widdows has carried out … a revolution in the planning and arrangement of school buildings … a real advance which

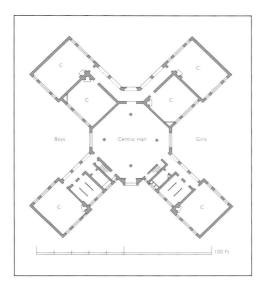

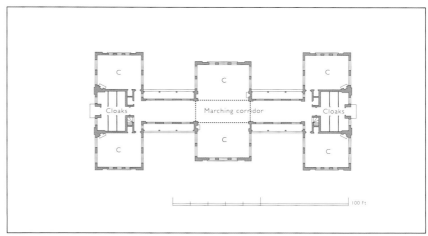

*Plans of Derbyshire schools by
George Widdows*

*Figure 58 (above)
Wirksworth Elementary School, 1912
[Based on* The Builder *1913,* **105***, 460]*

*Figure 59 (above, right)
Highfield Elementary School, Long Eaton,
1911
[Redrawn from Seaborne and Lowe 1977, 84,
and with permission from Derbyshire Record
Office]*

*Figure 60 (right)
Creswell Elementary School, 1912
[Based on* The Builder *1913,* **105***, 460]*

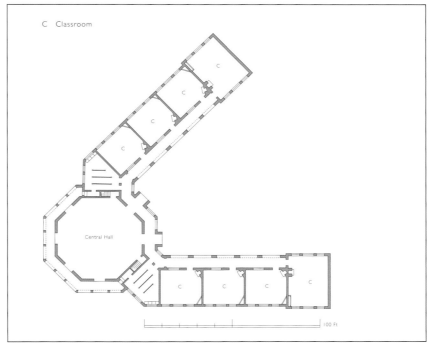

places English school architecture without a rival either in a European country or in the United States'.[9] The other progressive authority of the Edwardian period was Devon, where Percy Morris adapted a Widdows design as early as 1909 at Woolbrook, Sidmouth.

Figure 61
Croft Road School, Alfreton, 1907 by George Widdows for Derbyshire Education Committee, the best-preserved example of his butterfly planning.
[© Elain Harwood]

Open-air schools

Concern for health found its most extreme expression in the 'open air' movement for delicate and tubercular children. Their model was a school opened in August 1904 in a pine forest in the suburbs of Berlin at Charlottenburg. A report on it was published by the LCC in 1908, together with a study of its own experiment in the summer of 1907 on the Royal Arsenal Co-operative Society's open land in Bostall Wood, Woolwich (Fig 62). The programme of teaching, exercise, solid meals and afternoon rest came from Charlottenburg, where the school building comprised 'a plain shed 81ft long by 18ft wide completely open to the south' which was used for sleeping on wet afternoons, and two sheds open on all sides where meals were taken and which were used as classrooms in wet weather. Otherwise most lessons were taken in the open air. The experiment was declared a success despite inclement weather. The LCC's report showed that 'the short stay in the open air school stimulated the intellectual faculties and self reliance, encouraged by a course of instruction designed to raise an interest in nature'.[10] Tables show that the children grew several inches and gained considerably in weight, while letters from parents commended the caring attitude of the teachers. Further temporary schools followed in London, in huts imported from Christoph and Unmack's factory in Warsaw, evidence that the Charlottenburg model was imported lock, stock and barrel. The provision of school meals was itself pioneering, and breakfast, dinner and tea were provided. More permanent sites were developed with huts in the 1920s, including Aspen House in Brixton, developed with square classroom shelters, originally left unglazed.

Open-air schools were pioneered in Bradford by its City Architect, R G Kirkby, who built his first open-air school as early as 1907. Daisy Hill School, Bradford, of 1918 by W Williamson, had a dedicated block for the sick. In Bristol, Knowle School opened as an open-air school for sickly children in 1913. The buildings were closely modelled on the simple shelters found in isolation hospitals, and the pupils were expected to rest (usually on outdoor beds) in the afternoons. Bradford also pioneered the provision of school meals, begun in 1887 and developed by Margaret McMillan and the medical officers, first James Kerr and then Ralph Crowley, as a series of charitable 'Cinderella Clubs'. They inspired the Provision of School Meals Act in 1906, which

Figure 62 (opposite)
Reading class, London County Council open-air school, Bostall Wood, Woolwich, 1907.
[City of London, London Metropolitan Archives]

Figure 63 (right)
Green Lane School, Bradford, 1902. The kitchen, built in 1907 and restored in 2007, is at the rear of the site.
[Mike Williams]

permitted education authorities to run a meals service. Bradford opened the first kitchen at Green Lane School in 1907, whence lunches were distributed to other schools in the neighbourhood (Fig 63).

An obituary of Margaret McMillan in *The Labour Woman* for May 1931 described her as 'the most heroic figure in the world of education up to now' for her vision, oratory and persistent dedication to the cause of child health.[11] McMillan's work embodies the two great concerns of the early 20th century – for children's physical health and for mental stimulation. By 1900, 43.1 per cent of the population aged between three and five was in some form of schooling, usually so their mothers could work, and already educationalists were realising that normal school classes were tending to dull rather than encourage young children's minds. This became an issue as education began to become more than a matter of instruction by rote. In 1911 the Board of Education's retiring Chief Inspector, Edmond Holmes, launched an attack on 'blind, passive, mechanical obedience' in the classrooms, and a year later Maria Montessori's book, *The Method*, was translated into English.[12] Her ideas of learning through play and encouraging small children to think for themselves were based on a proven methodology developed in the slums of Rome. However, few nursery schools were built. Of those realised, the largest was by Rachel and Margaret McMillan in Deptford. It opened in 1914 in modest temporary shelters, with a curriculum based on open-air principles informed by the ideas of Edouard Séguin and Frederick Froebel. Margaret McMillan built a training college next door in 1929–30, and something of her influence can be seen in the movement towards light-weight, child-friendly structures that began in the 1930s.

Secondary education

The 1900s saw an expansion of secondary education. In 1902 there were 272 recognised secondary schools, largely inherited from the voluntary sector; by 1912 there were a thousand as Britain struggled belatedly to compete with the higher educational standards of the United States and Germany. They evolved in a very different way from the elementary schools, with most authorities emphasising status rather than health – admissible since these were buildings largely for children from better homes. The Board of Education encouraged a general education, without emphasis on science or the needs of local industry – a controversial move that set back vocational training for much of the century. A few new grammar schools were built in a late Queen Anne style, notably the King Edward VII School at King's Lynn, Norfolk, designed by Basil Champneys in 1906. But a symmetrical neo-Georgian style was generally preferred for its greater dignity and timelessness, appropriate to a secondary school and also the style by then being adopted by the older foundations which the local authorities sought to emulate. The Bromley Boys' Secondary School of 1911 by H P Burke Downing is a fine example, with an elaborate centrepiece fronting a large assembly hall, with long wings to either side. In Blyth, Northumberland, the secondary school was built to an 'early Georgian' style following a competition won by Edward Cratney, with boys to one side, girls to the other, in a symmetrical composition.

Elsewhere, more secondary schools began to be built for girls, to meet the demand for teachers. Pupil teachers were now made to attend secondary school full-time for at least a year, as was first implemented in Kent in 1906, by which time nine new schools had been built for girls in the county compared with three for boys. Huddersfield, West Yorkshire, built a new secondary school for girls in 1908, by which date the LCC had built 17, mainly for girls and

beginning with that at Hortensia Road, Chelsea, a four-storey building by T J Bailey still reminiscent of his board schools. A particularly fine example is that at Cassland Road, Hackney, from 1901–2, which is more architecturally ambitious than Bailey's mainstream board schools (Fig 64).

In Derbyshire, George Widdows brought his concern for ventilation and good health to secondary schools, arguing in 1910 that 'secondary buildings require just as much revolutionising as elementary. All one can say is there are not so many children in each class and their clothes do not stink.'[13] The outstanding example is Ilkeston Grammar School of 1911–14, a largely single-storey building with both classical and organic references in its detailing, where he set his accommodation round a courtyard, again with open verandahs providing the circulation and with a concrete domed hall in the centre, linked only by covered ways (p 50). Similar plans were adopted by many counties into the 1930s where land was available and, like the primaries, secondary schools also came to feature large windows.

6

A missed opportunity: inter-war schools, 1914–1940

The inter-war years saw many new ideas that went largely unrealised, due to the poor economy. The 1918 Education Act proposed a system of continuation schools and encouraged a national programme of education accessible 'to every person capable of profiting by it', but an economic downturn and a parsimonious government elected in 1921 ensured it had little effect. The 'Day Continuation' schools built in 1925 at Bournville, Birmingham, by S A Wilmot with the support of the Cadbury family, were rare responses to this clause. The Act's one legacy was to raise the school leaving age to 14, but such was the shortage of school places, building materials and funding after the war that many emergency classrooms were formed from wartime huts.

This period also saw the gradual evolution of a two-tier system of elementary and higher schools for children in local authority education, with a break at 11 years of age. The Hadow Report in 1926 recommended the building of 'senior elementary' or 'modern' schools to offer a general education that complemented the more academic grammar schools, and a further consultative committee, chaired by William Spens in 1938, proposed a third – technical – stream.[14] Junior technical schools had already begun to evolve with more purpose-built facilities for younger students. For the grammar schools in particular, a neo-Georgian style remained dominant. Sites on the edge of towns and cities meant that ample playing fields could be provided for sports and allowed for more expansive planning. Hadow emphasised the need for science laboratories for older children, and gymnasia with wall bars, beams and vaulting horses. New public day schools were built formally around quadrangles, and inspired similar designs from local authorities. One of the earliest and largest examples was in Bolton, Lancashire, designed by C T Adshead and built between 1918 and 1929, its vast scale made possible by generous donations from W H Lever. The King George V Grammar School at Southport, Lancashire, built by Julian Leathart and W F Grainger from 1924 onwards, demonstrated what could be achieved on a humbler budget, while High Storrs School, Sheffield, of 1933, is minimally classical (Fig 65). Writing in 1940, Leathart showed that secondary schools tended still to be neo-Georgian in style, perhaps with a Scandinavian influence to features like a clock tower. More progressive designs were reserved for technical schools, as found in the Germanic mouldings of Stretford's Junior Technical School completed that year, a contrast to the earlier classical grammar school by the same architect, Stephen Wilkinson.[15]

Joicey Road Open Air School, Gateshead, realised in 1936–7 to designs by the Borough Engineer's Department. The classrooms, for 150 boys and girls, were arranged on a staggered plan to give a maximum of sunshine and have large folding windows on three sides. [AA040284]

The 1911 and 1921 Education Acts exempted new school buildings from local bye-laws, and in 1925 the Baines Committee recommended building more cheaply, suggesting that corridors and halls be reduced and roofs set at a lower pitch. Its report was never published, but informed the Board of Education's advocacy of lightweight buildings (Fig 66). When in 1931 Middlesex County Council, confronted by London's rapid westward advancement, cut building budgets by 30 per cent, the incoming County Architect, W T Curtis, and his assistant H W Burchett, turned to steel framing, which coincidentally gave them a greater planning flexibility than traditional construction. They were particularly impressed by the brick and steel schools built by Willem Dudok,

Figure 65
A stripped-down neo-Georgian style was commonly used for grammar schools in the inter-war years, because it gave an image of tradition and dignity at modest cost. This is High Storrs Grammar School, Sheffield, of 1933 by the City Architect's Department.
[Mike Williams]

director of public works in Hilversum (the Netherlands' new garden city), and himself inspired by Frank Lloyd Wright. Dudok countered the long horizontal glazing patterns inevitable in classroom wings by the cubic massing of taller ranges and the vertical accent of a glazed stair tower. His influence can be seen, sometimes on an enormous scale, in Middlesex's secondary schools such as Greenford High School of 1937; simpler and more dynamic are the primary

Figure 67 (left)
Lady Bankes School, Pinner, built in 1936 (opened in 1937) by Middlesex County Council architects, under W T Curtis and H W Burchett.
[© Elain Harwood]

Figure 68 (above)
Doncaster Grammar (now Hall Cross) School (W Yorks), a school of the 1880s extended by Leathart and Grainger in 1938 in the style made fashionable in the Netherlands by Willem Dudok.
[Mike Williams]

schools, Lady Bankes, Pinner (Fig 67), and De Bohun, Enfield, both of 1936. Leathart and Grainger provided an extension in 1938 to Doncaster Grammar School, West Yorkshire, in a similar style but to a higher budget (Fig 68). These schools are typical of the short burst of school building in the late 1930s, as authorities frantically tried to make up a shortfall of places – the result of two decades of little building and mass migration, particularly of skilled workers to and within the Midlands and the South East.

Open-air schools were built in greater numbers (Fig 69). Even where the structures were substantially of brick, one classroom wall would be retractable, as at Joicey Road Open Air School in Gateshead, County Durham, first planned in 1924 but not realised until 1936–7 (p 62). Lessons could be taken inside or out. Meanwhile new research suggested that children's eyesight was being

Figure 69
Drill at Charlton Park Open Air School, Woolwich,
built by the London County Council in 1929–30.
[City of London, London Metropolitan Archives]

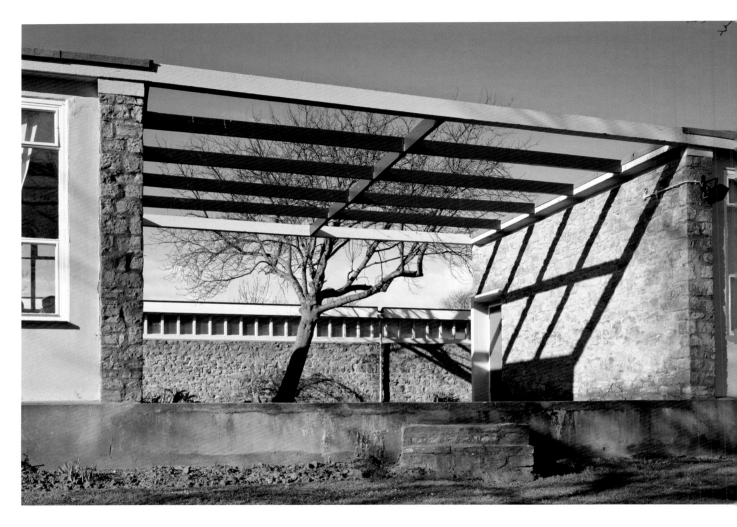

Figure 70
Former Richmond High School for Girls, Richmond (N Yorks), built in 1938–40 to designs by Denis Clarke Hall using local stone in a modernist design that paid special attention to natural daylighting, hence the stretched-out plan with its internal courtyards.
[Mike Williams]

harmed by poor school lighting, and a glazed wall with some corresponding clerestory lighting from the opposite side became an important factor in school design. This could be readily achieved by steel frame construction, using a 'finger plan' of single-storey classrooms in long ranges reached off a lower corridor. At Sussex, C G Stillman worked with a local caravan manufacturer to prefabricate a light-weight steel system in 8ft 3in lengths; three of these units made a standard classroom, and any number could be put end to end. A prototype at Sidlesham, West Sussex, in 1936 marked the first major use of prefabrication in school building.

Interest in school design was further fostered with a competition run by the *News Chronicle* in 1937. This was for two 'senior mixed elementary schools' for children between the ages of 11 and 14. It is ironic that at a time when better qualified and more imaginative architects were being attracted to public offices, the competition enabled a young generation in private practice to make their careers designing schools. The urban category was won by Denis Clarke Hall and a version was built as the Richmond High School for Girls, North Yorkshire, in 1938–40, introducing a tempered modernism using local stone (Fig 70).

A few small progressive independent schools were founded in the 1920s. A handful of boarding schools offered working-class children a new life outside the cities, including the Caldecott Community in Kent and Tiptree Hall in Essex. The first Steiner school, based on the philosophy of Austrian educationalist Rudolf Steiner – a topic-based learning that encourages children to be creative – was founded in Streatham, London, in 1925. Middle-class schools took over the large country estates then coming on to the market, including Stowe (Buckinghamshire), Bryanston (Dorset), and Dartington in Devon, where a school was built in 1926 under the patronage of Dorothy and Leonard Elmhurst. In 1929 William B Curry from Philadelphia became headmaster of Dartington and invited over his architect William Lescaze. The houses and dormitories built by Lescaze and Robert Hening in 1931–4 were among the first examples of the international modern style in Britain (Fig 71). The burgeoning interests in modern architecture and new teaching ideas came together in the nursery movement. Light-weight, highly glazed buildings offered a freshness and informality thought to stimulate young minds. In 1934 the Nursery Schools Association commissioned Ernö Goldfinger to design a prototype nursery classroom in timber, while Leslie Martin and Sadie Speight produced an elegant example with a covered verandah for a Quaker benefactress at Hartford, Cheshire, in 1938. The modern idiom of concrete or white painted brick was also sometimes used for ancillary buildings such as domestic science centres. A domestic science block at Ilford, Essex, built in 1937 in a modern style, incorporated a model flat in which schoolgirls could practice housewifery. At established public schools a modern style was seen as appropriate for science laboratories, then being built in some numbers as the need to keep up with technical advances in Europe and the United States became recognised. W G Newton designed a strongly neo-Georgian Memorial Hall in 1921–5 at Marlborough College in Wiltshire, but adopted a truly modern idiom in exposed concrete with large areas of glass for the Science Building, opened in 1933 (Fig 72).

Figure 72
Science Building, Marlborough College (Wilts), built by
W G Newton in 1933. The modern style was thought
appropriate for science while other new buildings at the
school were still firmly traditional.
[© Elain Harwood]

Figure 73
Impington Village College (Cambs),
by Walter Gropius, 1938–9.
[© Elain Harwood]

From 1920 George Widdows produced experimental designs for village schools with large halls which could be used for social events outside school hours. That schools could bring a social and cultural stimulus to rural areas facing progressive emaciation by emigration to the towns was recognised more fully by Henry Morris, the Secretary for Education for Cambridgeshire. He built four village colleges in the 1930s, to be community centres that 'a child would enter at three and leave only in extreme old age': Sawston, Bottisham, Linton and Impington (opened in 1930, 1937, 1938 and 1939 respectively).[16] Together with further examples in the 1950s, they influenced the idea of continuation schools or 'county colleges' as developed in the early 1960s. Architecturally, however, it was only Impington which received attention, because its simple, rational brick design was the major work of Walter Gropius during his stay in England between 1934 and 1938 (Fig 73).

7

Education for all, 1945–1985

One in five schools in England and Wales were destroyed or badly damaged in the Second World War. Planning for new schools began in 1943 and led to the reorganisation of secondary education in 1944. This was based on the premise that a falling population needed to be educated to the maximum of its abilities. What was not recognised until 1946 was that the birth rate had begun to rise dramatically, and only declined from the mid-1960s. The first post-war demand was thus for infant places in those suburban areas where new schools had failed to keep up with housing and light industry in the 1930s (Fig 74). There was still greater pressure in Middlesex, Essex and especially Hertfordshire, where new estates and new towns were built for London's evacuees, meaning that some 10 new schools were needed every year.

Prefabricated schools

The Ministry of Education in 1943 recommended the use of standardised prefabricated components and, following expenditure cuts in 1949, committed every authority to a three-year building plan that was carefully costed.[17]

(opposite)
Sydenham School, Dartmouth Road, London. Large additions of 1957 by Basil Spence and Partners to convert an old grammar school to a comprehensive are good examples of the style of the period (see also front cover).
[DP059424].

Figure 74 (right)
High Leys Infant School, Hucknall, Nottinghamshire County Council, 1948. An example of a traditionally built post-war school, with large windows on to an outdoor teaching area.
[Nottinghamshire Archives, CC/ED/11/4/31]

Hertfordshire adapted a light steel-framed system – developed by Hills of West Bromwich for wartime huts – into a rational method of building elementary schools (Fig 75). Austere externally, windows were made low so the smallest child could see out. There were tiled areas for messing with paints and glue; small desks, chairs, sinks, toilets, and coat pegs were purpose-designed. Bright colour schemes, sculptures and murals gave stimulus and pleasure for the first time in a consistent programme.

Similar prefabricated systems, usually privately manufactured, were taken up by other authorities, notably Lancashire and the LCC. The motivator from Hertfordshire, Stirrat Johnson-Marshall, set up a research unit at the Ministry of Education in 1948, where he experimented with these systems in collaboration with sympathetic authorities such as Coventry. Most prefabricated systems were only suited to single-storey building, and were inappropriate for large secondary schools. The Ministry set to change this, experimenting with steel at St Crispin's, Wokingham, Berkshire (1951–3, Fig 76), with aluminium at Lyng Hall and Whitley Abbey in Coventry, and with

Figure 75
Essendon School, by Bill Henderson and Dan Lacey of Hertfordshire County Council, the second of their prefabricated schools in 1947–8.
[© Elain Harwood]

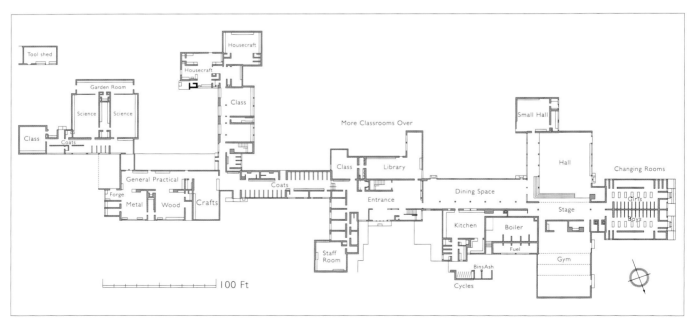

Figure 76 (opposite)
St Crispin's, Wokingham (Berks), designed in 1949–50
by Mary and David Medd and Michael Ventris, and
opened in 1953. It pushed the use of Hills' hot-rolled steel
system to three storeys, and was a model plan for the new
secondary modern schools then promoted by the Ministry
of Education with a large area for crafts. The plan
influenced so many suburban schools in England and
Wales that it now appears ordinary.
[Based on Ministry of Education 1952, Building Bulletin
8, App 8]

Figure 77 (above)
Intake (originally Bancroft Lane) School, Mansfield,
1955–6. This was Nottinghamshire's first school built
using the CLASP system. Its system of spring-loaded
foundations, designed to ride mining subsidence, in 1956
earned it the title 'the rock and roll school'.
[© Elain Harwood]

concrete at Durrington, Worthing, Sussex. However, the most successful of all the prefabricated systems was designed not only for all types of schools but also for a wide range of public buildings. It was (and remains) that devised to tolerate mining subsidence by Donald Gibson for Nottinghamshire County Council. CLASP is a pin-jointed and spring-loaded light steel frame at first clad with timber and tiles giving it a vernacular quality, lost in later versions that used concrete panels. To ease the cost of its development Gibson brought together a group of education authorities that faced similar problems – hence its name, the Consortium of Local Authorities Special Programme. Variations of CLASP were used for York University and in housing, as well as for hundreds of schools, but its greatest influence was on the organisation of education authorities into building consortia (Fig 77).

Comprehensive schools

The three-tier system of grammar, technical grammar and secondary modern schools was finally adopted with the passing of R A Butler's Education Act of 1944. At last sufficient secondary schools would be built to give every child a proper secondary education. The new grammar and technical schools were

simplified versions of existing models, the latter with larger workshop blocks. But no models existed for the secondary moderns. At the Ministry of Education the architects Mary and David Medd suggested an informal design, with a tower of conventional classrooms and single-storey studios for vocational training, realised at St Crispin's, Wokingham. The Smithsons won a

Figure 78
Elliott School, Roehampton. This is perhaps the finest of the large comprehensive schools built by the London County Council Architect's Department (group leader George Trevett). Built in 1954–6, it has an eclectic range of modern materials and details.
[© Elain Harwood]

competition to design Hunstanton School, Norfolk, with a formal two-storey scheme set around two courtyards divided by a central hall.

The tripartite system offered too little, too late, for the most progressive educationalists. The intelligence testing which determined a child's career at age 11 seemed iniquitous to progressive authorities like London, Middlesex, Birmingham and Coventry, while in rural areas the cost of building and equipping three schools was unrealistic. The North and East Ridings, and small urban authorities, proposed 'bilateral' schools combining two of the three elements. Others built all three types of school on a single site. In 1944 the LCC recommended a 'multilateral' approach of combining all three elements in one unit (p 72), a policy confirmed in its *London School Plan* of 1947 and adopted also by Coventry. A problem with these new comprehensive schools was the size required to sustain a lively sixth form, estimated by the Ministry at 2,000 children. In Coventry, schools were built in small units or 'houses', each creating a close-knit environment for a cross-section of children within the school; in London, where land was limited, vast single blocks were built, often with only halls and/or workshop areas set separately. Elliott School, Roehampton, London Borough of Wandsworth is a good example from 1954–6 (Fig 78), its steel framed main block lightly clad with glass curtain walling and a jaunty mix of details indebted to both the Bauhaus and the Festival of Britain. Where grammar schools already existed the LCC built small 'county complements', secondary moderns but with decent science and art rooms. Rutherford School, St Marylebone, by Leonard Manasseh combined all these facilities in a single block, defined by its structural concrete mullions and topped by an inverted pyramid watertank. It has now been remodelled as part of the King Solomon Academy.

The first authority to challenge the established separation of primary and secondary schooling was Leicestershire. In 1957 it introduced a plan to convert its 'secondary modern' stock into schools for those aged between 11 and 14, so that all the older children could use the better-equipped grammar and technical schools. As new schools came to be built at Desford (1967–70, Fig 79), Syston (1967–71), both by Gollins Melvin Ward, and at Countesthorpe by Farmer and Dark (1967–70, Figs 80 and 81), so conventions were further challenged by more flexible, centralised plans. Classrooms were replaced by open teaching areas grouped round a library or resource centre, and science

Figure 79
Bosworth Community College, Desford (Leics), 1967–70 by Gollins, Melvin, Ward and Partners, the first of the county's purpose-built upper schools. The sculpture, by Bernard Schottlander, was purchased as part of the capital programme, which included a percentage for art. [Mike Williams].

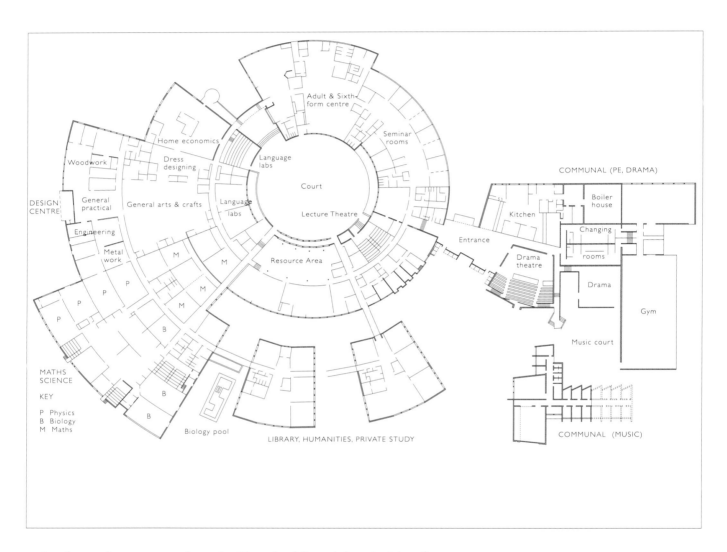

Within the figure (labels):

Adult & Sixth-form centre
Home economics
Dress designing
Woodwork
Language labs
Seminar rooms
COMMUNAL (PE, DRAMA)
Court
Boiler house
DESIGN CENTRE
General practical
General arts & crafts
Language labs
Lecture Theatre
Kitchen
Changing rooms
Engineering
Metal work
Resource Area
Entrance
Drama theatre
Drama
Gym
P
M
Music court
B
MATHS SCIENCE
KEY
P Physics
B Biology
M Maths
Biology pool
LIBRARY, HUMANITIES, PRIVATE STUDY
COMMUNAL (MUSIC)

and craft areas became open plan units. They also followed the principles of Henry Morris's Cambridgeshire village colleges in providing facilities for the entire community. In Nottinghamshire comprehensive schools were grouped with community sports centres, as at Sutton-in-Ashfield (1972–6) and Chilwell

Figure 80
Countesthorpe Community College
[Based on Architectural Review *1971,* **150***, 8]*

Figure 81
Countesthorpe Community College,
a section of the exterior.
[Mike Williams]

(1969–79). Other authorities, notably West Yorkshire and Bradford, made an educational break at age 9, establishing 'middle schools' for those aged 9–13. Where new buildings were required here they tended to be compact single-storey structures that combined classrooms with shared areas for study, group working, art and science. However, reorganisation following the introduction of the national curriculum means that few middle schools survive.

Open planning

Open planning was widely adopted by primary schools, particularly in rural areas where small classes had to embrace a broad age range. The Department of Education and Science (DES) pioneered two such schools in 1958–9, at Finmere, Oxfordshire, and Great Ponton, Lincolnshire. More influential still was a DES prototype for urban areas, Eveline Lowe in Peckham, developed in 1963–6 for children aged 3–9 years, with grouped activity areas, quiet rooms and home bases serving broad age ranges. In Leicestershire primaries, open teaching areas were gathered round a central library, quiet study room or assembly area, sometimes on a circular plan, sometimes in the form of pavilions. Both plan types were included as models for other authorities in the DES 1967 report *Children and their Primary Schools*. Examples of open planning can be seen in the later work of Birkin Haward in Ipswich and Jack Digby in West Suffolk.

Some of these schools employed building systems, and by 1966 most English education authorities belonged to one of eight consortia – Buckinghamshire and Northamptonshire were the principal exceptions. But by the 1970s architects were reporting these systems to be increasingly restrictive and no longer economical. The Greater London Council – following a protest led by Louis Hellman, working there while establishing himself as a cartoonist – was in 1973 the first to abandon its system, MACE (Metropolitan Architectural Consortium for Education), after completing one comprehensive and a few primary schools.[18] Slowly authorities began to reassert their own distinctive styles, most notably in Hampshire, where Colin Stansfield Smith served as County Architect between 1974 and 1992. In the primary schools distinct classroom spaces are set around shared activity and circulation areas

Figure 82
Hatch Warren Infant School, Basingstoke, 1984 by Stephen Harte and Terry Riggs of Hampshire County Council Architect's Department, showing the deep, split-level plan with its common central areas lit from above.
[© Elain Harwood]

Figure 83
Fort Hill Community School, Basingstoke, 1972–6
by Trevor Harris, John Laye and Peter Galloway of
Hampshire County Council Architect's Department.
It reacted against the county's prefabricated system with
a return to traditional materials, setting low buildings
around a courtyard.
[© Elain Harwood]

that maximised the economies of a deep plan (Fig 82). A few of the schools used bright steel frames, but most were designed as a modern interpretation of a historic barn cast adrift in a sea of suburbia, with brightly tiled roofs, high clerestories and clunky timber detailing. The secondary schools tended to be longer and lower, with accommodation set off a central courtyard or atrium (Fig 83). These schools were among the first to tackle the problems of solar gain and heat loss identified in earlier post-war schools constructed of lighter materials, and their plans are repeated in the new wave of schools being built in the 21st century.

8

Guidance for selection for listing

What listing means

Governors and local authorities may fear the listing of their schools as restrictive, but such concerns are usually founded on a mistaken belief that listing will prevent necessary change and the updating of facilities. Listing is not designed to freeze buildings. Its main purpose is to ensure that the architectural and historic interest of a building is taken into account when proposals are made to alter or demolish it. We need to understand our historic buildings before sensible decisions can be made about their future. A school needs to be judged against its appropriate peers – a village school usually has different attributes from an urban one – and the criteria vary according to the age and type of school. Schools are important community assets, but listing can only take architectural and historical claims into account. Almost all the schools illustrated in this book are listed, save the most recent.

Criteria

Most school buildings from before the reorganisation of the mid-1830s, if they survive in their original form, will be listed already. All schools built before 1870 should be considered, but examples have to be well preserved and of good quality to be listed. The most innovatory schools of these periods will be eligible for high grades, as will be the architecturally sophisticated and many of those designed by architects of national repute. Nevertheless, even the humblest school is worthy of consideration if it retains its original form, and especially if it retains internal fittings. The most modest schools can be identified by dedicatory plaques even where there have been subsequent alterations. Unfortunately, these plaques were often reused if the school was rebuilt or extended and are not conclusive proof of an early date.

Far greater care is needed in assessing the vast number of board schools erected after 1870. Two main factors determine listability, the quality of the external architecture and the degree of completeness (Fig 84). A careful assessment has to be made to see if the building was completed as intended, that its original form remains recognisable, and that any extensions are not detrimental. Internal plans are likely to have been altered, though glazed

Fairlawn School, Honor Oak, Lewisham, by Peter Moro for the London County Council, 1955–7. A three-storey block for juniors is contrasted with a loosely planned single-storey range for infants. This school was listed in 2008 for the quiet sophistication of its elevations and attention to detail, particularly in its well-preserved interiors.
[DP059340]

Figure 84
London: Bellenden Road School, Southwark,
1876–7, an example of E R Robson's mature style.
[© Elain Harwood]

sliding screens may indicate traditional arrangements. Internal components
tend to be simple but attractive, with bold roof trusses to achieve the wide roof
spans, strong joinery and glazed brickwork. A decision to list is unlikely to be
dependent on such elements but they are always worthy of retention. It is
important that external characteristics survive intact, since chimneys and gable
copings that are reduced or simplified in the name of economy debase
architectural quality. Schools that are imaginatively designed will inevitably
be chosen over plain, utilitarian examples. Early Gothic style schools will usually
be asymmetrical, even picturesque, compositions while later board schools were

Figure 85
Bradford: Byron Street, 1897 by C M Hargreaves
[© Elain Harwood]

generally intended to be symmetrical, but were sometimes not completed (Fig 85). Later schools may be very large and repetitive, and need to be carefully considered in comparison with other examples. Though often prominent landmarks – especially when set amidst small terraced houses – these buildings should always be assessed in a national context (Fig 86). Ancillary buildings should always be looked for: high-quality walls, railings and gates may contribute significantly to the architectural impact of a school group, as can buildings for domestic science, covered playgrounds, toilet blocks and a master's house. When complete, these complexes can support the case for listing.

Open-air schools were built in significant numbers either side of the First World War. This was no isolated fad, but a deep-rooted social movement that influenced school design into the 1960s. However, as at the Rachel McMillan School (*see* pp 59–60), many of the huts were always intended to be temporary, while elsewhere they were so light and flimsy that few survive. In the 1920s it is necessary to separate schools that incorporated a few ideas about cross ventilation from more thorough-going experiments in open-air teaching. These examples are much rarer and are always worthy of detailed research for listing.

Thresholds for listing are higher for more recent buildings. Schools from the 1920s were often built to a more ambitious scale on larger sites, with more specialist teaching rooms. The traditionally styled buildings are often architecturally very imposing, and here the quality of the external design has to be assessed with the survival of internal contemporary features. These include panelling in the principal spaces and head teacher's room, fitted furnishings and the survival of libraries, science laboratories and specialised facilities. In public schools these may be in a variety of styles. Many secondary schools have stained glass or murals, often as a war memorial to former scholars lost in the First World War. While frequently well-built and dignified in design, special architectural interest is not always apparent, and selection is necessary. Still more difficult to assess are the large number of Dudok-inspired modernist schools, for only the most boldly massed and complete are likely to be of special interest – staircase towers form particularly interesting features. Schools which have been greatly extended, or which have lost their original windows, roofs and other contemporary features, are unlikely to be listable. Examples of Modern Movement architecture are rare and likely to be small in scale; many are already listed.

The post-war period saw schools take a lead in public funding, such was the demand for places and the importance given to education. Yet although school building occupied a privileged place and was at the forefront of innovation, examples from less than 40 sites, or 13.35 per cent of the total listings of the period, are so far listed. The strictest selection is necessary because so many schools were built during this time (p 82). Many of the most interesting primary schools date from the years between 1948 and 1951, when the budgets were highest and enthusiasm greatest. The most inspired county was Hertfordshire. While its schools used standard components, there is a wide diversity in massing that made some more architecturally successful than others. Look for the survival of original child-size fittings and works of art. The best primary schools reflect the small scale of their clients, and their architecture is consequently modest and intimate without grand gestures. Hertfordshire's zealous spirit inspired later county programmes, notably in Nottinghamshire, Leicestershire and Hampshire, but individual primary schools around the country can be innovatory in their construction or plan form, or in taking particular account of a local setting. Schools built for those with special needs have again to be assessed on an individual basis, such is their diversity. There is an exceptionally low survival rate as requirements have changed most markedly in this area.

Secondary schools are much larger and more conventionally architectural, but again many have been heavily altered as educational policies have changed. The most interesting examples took on a challenging brief – such as to provide the wide range of facilities required for comprehensive education or evening classes (perhaps as a village college) – or had to adapt to a difficult site. It is crucial that the building works as a total entity, and that it displays special features or a cohesion of ideas that sets it apart from its peers. The authorities with the most distinctive secondary building programmes were London, Coventry, Leicestershire, Hampshire and the many small authorities building in the Black Country. Despite attempts at standardisation in secondary schools, one-off designs remained more important than strict adherence to a system.

Figure 86
Tottenham: Nightingale Primary School, Bounds
Green Road, 1899 by Mitchell and Butler as a
higher grade school.
[© Elain Harwood]

9

Conclusion: new uses for old schools

Schools are among the oldest of building types, and considerable numbers survive from the Middle Ages and post-Reformation years. The preservation of such striking buildings in some benign use is generally assured, as is that of the still larger numbers of 17th- and 18th-century schools. But schools of the 19th and particularly the 20th centuries are under threat as never before, although their historic importance is as great – for they demonstrate how education was brought within the means of us all – and many are architecturally imposing. This book has tried to show what makes some schools particularly special, by assessing their architectural features within a historical context. Yet all schools have some interest and, whether listed or not, they can be adapted for continued educational service or put to a new use.

Case studies

It is inevitable as people age in an area, or move away, that school rolls will rise and fall, and that some buildings will fall out of use. But school buildings – particularly older ones with their large, high-ceilinged classrooms – are loose and flexible shapes suitable for a variety of uses. A stay of execution for St George's Schools in Bolton, Lancashire, built in 1847, will hopefully save this advanced Jacobean design from demolition, while a Public Enquiry in 2007 found in favour of the retention of J Morson's imposing schools of 1911–13 in Easington, County Durham (Fig 87).

Buildings refurbished for continued school use

The best use for a building is generally that for which it is designed, as first formally set out in the government's Planning Policy Guidance Note 15, and this should be taken into account when considering a school's future, whether or not it is listed.[19] Reading is an excellent example of a local authority that has kept virtually all its schools in use, ranging from All Saints church school of 1865 to board schools in a variety of styles, including Gothic Revival by Joseph Morris from the 1870s and more severe Queen Anne by S S Stallwood, sometimes with large chimneys serving an air extraction or 'plenum' system. A comprehensive master plan may help determine a strategy for the continued use and extension of a historic school building, as was

Braunton Board School (Devon), begun in 1873 and undergoing extension in 2009.
[DP082391]

Figure 88 (left)
The entrance hall of Lansbury Lawrence Primary School,
Cordelia Street, Tower Hamlets (1949–50). The colourful
tiles by Peggy Angus are part of the Festival of Britain
detailing that makes this school so special. The school has
recently been refurbished, and the hall reinstated as the
school's main entrance.
[DP059457]

Figure 89 (right)
The Burlington Danes Academy, in Hammersmith,
is an unusually lavish school by Burnet, Tait and Lorne
(1935–7) and indebted to Dutch design. The new block
added in 2007–8 by Barnsley Hewett and Mallinson is
modern yet respectful.
[© Elain Harwood]

Figure 90 (below)
Awsworth Infants' School (Notts), 1895,
now a nursery school.
[© Elain Harwood]

found by Bishop Wordsworth School in Salisbury, Wiltshire, sensitively located in the Cathedral Close. Another important case was that of the grade I listed Sir John Moore's school at Appleby Magna, Leicestershire, restored for school use in 2003.

Board schools were often built in phases, for example that at Braunton, Devon, built in 1873 and extended in the 1880s with further gables (p 88). That this tradition can be continued is shown by the new extension approved by English Heritage and due for completion in 2009. As well as winning awards for its new schools, Hampshire Architect's Department has developed expertise in extending its schools, whether in a traditional style as at Burley Primary School (1997) or using lightweight steel, as at Westgate School, Winchester (1993). That additions can often be radically different from the original building is demonstrated by the learning resources centre added in 2004 by IID Architects to the Tiffin School, Kingston-upon-Thames, a drum of glass and steel that makes a striking contrast to the brickwork of the listed building, an 18th-century converted house.

Buildings from the 20th century can also be adapted very successfully. A post-war school recently refurbished is Lansbury Lawrence Primary School. This complex was built as the Susan Lawrence Primary and Elizabeth Lansbury Nursery Schools by Yorke, Rosenberg and Mardall in 1949–52, when it formed part of the 'Live' architecture exhibition of the Festival of Britain. The buildings were listed grade II in 1998. In 2006–7 a new classroom wing was discretely added, a library created in the original building, and the neglected entrance hall was brought back into use. As part of this programme the school's striking tile murals by Peggy Angus were cleaned and restored (Fig 88). For secondary school children, the Burlington Danes Academy in Hammersmith, designated in 2006, occupies a Church of England girls' school built by Burnet, Tait and Lorne in 1935–7 (Fig 89). The listed building in the style of Willem Dudok has been beautifully restored, and a new block containing 16 classrooms and 4 laboratories was added in 2007–8 by Barnsley Hewett and Mallinson.

Older schools no longer required for teaching older children may often be successfully adapted as nurseries, as exemplified by listed Awsworth Infants' School (Fig 90), ideal because of its central location in the village and the enclosed playground. In Ilford, Essex, the domestic science block (grade II) added to Uphall Elementary School by the Ilford Borough Council

Figure 91
The domestic science block at Uphall School, built in 1937 by Ilford Borough Council, was adapted as a nursery in 1999 by Tooley and Foster.
[© Elain Harwood]

Architect's Department in 1937 was adapted as a nursery in 1999 by Tooley and Foster, who dropped ceilings and added porthole windows at a child's eye level that are in keeping with the building's ocean-liner style (Fig 91).

Schools converted to other uses

Where school use is no longer an option, school buildings can be adapted for a variety of new uses (Fig 92). The most attractive conversions of school buildings are into other public uses (Fig 93). This was demonstrated early by Liverpool's Blue Coat School, which closed in 1906 and was occupied briefly by the city's School of Architecture before becoming a library and arts centre, and more recently a gallery and workshops. St John's School in Chester (1810) has been converted to a visitor centre, as have the Roe Street Schools in Macclesfield, Cheshire. At Corsham, Wiltshire, two adjoining schools have been remodelled as the Pound Art Centre, opened in 2007 after a £1.25 million refurbishment (Fig 94). The 1839 British School has been converted to a 100-seat performance space, and a glazed walkway now links it to the main centre across the playground in the former board school of 1895. In Birmingham, the

Oozells Street School of 1877–8 by Martin and Chamberlain was refurbished as an arts venue, opening as the Ikon Gallery in 1998 (*frontispiece*). All Saints Primary School in Cockermouth, Cumbria, was converted to a community arts centre, auditorium and museum as early as 1994. Ipswich's Bramford Road Board School, by Brightwen Binyon from 1882 and extended in 1888 by E Fernley Bissopp, was converted in the 1980s into the East Suffolk Record Office, retaining the two halls as reading rooms.

Victorian and Edwardian schools convert readily to offices because of their high ceilings and stout construction. In Leeds, the Higher Grade School in Great George Street of 1899 by Birchall and Kelly, and the adjoining pupil teacher college of 1900 by W S Braithwaite, were converted to council offices in 1994–5 by Leeds Design Consultancy without disturbing the exteriors. The Harehills School of 1897, which closed in 1986 and was saved from demolition in 2000, is now being converted by the Camberwell Project to a business and conference centre, 'Shine'. The Camberwell Project created the Harehills Community Interest Company in 2007 to ensure the building cannot be sold for profit but will remain in social use. In Windsor, St Steven's School, built to the designs of

Figure 92 (above, left)
Taunton's School, Highfield Road, Southampton, 1926 by Gutteridge and Gutteridge, has been successfully adapted for use by the nearby university.
[© Elain Harwood]

Figure 93 (above)
British Schools at Hitchin (Herts), rebuilt in 1837 by Joseph Lancaster, with a galleried schoolroom added in 1853. The complex is now a museum, regularly used for re-enactments of Victorian school life.
[K980207]

Figure 94 (above)
Corsham Board School (Wilts), 1895, refurbished in
2007–8 as an arts centre and café.
[DP059578]

Figure 95 (above, right)
Ouseburn School, Newcastle, 1893 by F W Rich, sits in the
heart of a regeneration area by the River Tyne, the 17th-
century detailing conceals its stair and ventilation towers
– a contrast to the new buildings springing up around it.
[DP059477]

Henry Woodyer in 1876, has been adapted and extended as offices for 16 small businesses, while in Birmingham the Garrison Lane School has been converted to workshops. The Ouseburn School in Newcastle, an imposing design by Frank Rich from 1893, has been converted into a business centre – providing 47 offices and workshops for new businesses (Fig 95). In Folkestone, Kent, meanwhile, the Harvey Grammar School of 1895 was bought at auction in 1993 by the Grace Independent Baptist Church, which has adapted it as a chapel, Sunday school and social centre. A more boisterous use is that for Leonard Stoke's Oxford Boys Central School (1900–1) in Gloucester Green, Oxford, now a public house.

In rural areas very large numbers of schools have been converted to private houses. Larger urban schools can be converted readily to flats, and in many areas are popular – even trendy – although domestic curtaining can appear out

Figure 96 (above)
Stoneygate School, London Road, Leicester, an independent school in the Gothic style, was built in 1859, probably by Henry Goddard. It was converted to eight flats in 2003 by local builders William Davis.
[© Elain Harwood]

Figure 97 (left)
Former York Way Board School, London, built in 1873–4 by T W Aldwinkle in a Gothic style, largely rebuilt in 1910 and converted to flats in the 1990s.
[© Elain Harwood]

of place, and the imposition of mezzanines into the structure can be difficult (Figs 96 and 97). Such conversions can revive a depopulated neighbourhood, as in Ellesmere Port, Cheshire, where the John Street School was a good example of an early county council school designed to a healthy, single-storey plan as recommended by George Reid. It was built in 1911–12, perhaps to the designs of Charles E Deacon and Horsburgh of Liverpool, although it is rather different in style to the firm's other schools, and was listed grade II in late 1997. Poorly adapted as offices in the late 1960s, in *c* 2000 the school was converted to housing by the Wirral Methodist Housing Association in a well-designed scheme making attractive housing units as the double height classrooms had room for a mezzanine that provided bedroom space.

English Heritage saved the Latchmere Road Board Schools in Battersea, London Borrough of Wandsworth, from demolition in *c* 1990 by adding them to the adjoining Conservation Area using powers inherited from the Greater London Council. Though not themselves listable, the schools are interesting in that they show the work of E R Robson and T J Bailey side by side; the 'triple decker' from 1883 is Robson's last work, while the infants' school is a rare single-storey design of 1891. The schools were adapted into some 30 loft-style apartments in 1997 by developers Sapcote Real Lofts of Birmingham. Converting schools into flats has become very popular in London. A recent example is the former Kingsway College Clerkenwell Centre (originally the Hugh Myddelton Higher School), Islington, a lavish example of Bailey's work from 1892 that was built around the Middlesex House of Detention from 1845–7. In Manchester the Sheena Simon College remains partly in educational use, but one wing has been converted to flats, the dual use giving it a more secure future.

There are very many school buildings which are admired and even loved, and they have played an important role in their community. Few other buildings are so significant in so many lives. Such valuable storehouses of history deserve to be better understood, and, most importantly, they deserve to be reused. If this book helps the preservation of just one school it will have served its purpose.

Notes

1   Conan Doyle, Sir A 1893 'The naval treaty'. *The Strand*, Oct-Nov

2   Counties cited in this text are prior to the county boundary changes in 1974

3   Bell, A 1797 *An Experiment in Education, made at the Male Asylum of Madras*. London: Cadell and Davies; further edns 1805, 1807, 1812, 1813

4   Russell, R C 1960 A *History of Schools and Education in Barton-on-Humber, Part 1: 1800–1850*. Barton: Workers' Educational Association, 850

5   *The Builder*, **66**, 23 June 1894, 482

6   Quoted in Gill, A 'The Leicester School Board 1871–1903' *in* Simon, B (ed) 1968 *Education in Leicestershire, 1540–1940*. Leicester: Leicestershire University Press

7   Robson, E R 1872 'School planning'. *The Builder*, **30**, 6 July, 525

8   *Pall Mall Gazette*, **9234**, 27 October 1894

9   'The Derbyshire schools'. *The Builder*, **105**, 31 Oct 1913, 460

10 London County Council, Education Committee 1907 *Open-Air School, Bostall Wood (Plumstead)*. Report on experiments conducted in Germany in connection with open-air schools, and a joint report of the medical officer and the executive officer on experiments carried out at the Open-Air School in Bostall Wood between 22 July and 19 October 1907. London County Council

11 Leach, W, MP 1931 *in The Labour Woman*, 19 May, 68. Source: Margaret McMillan archives, 7/65, Lewisham Local Studies Library

12 Holmes, E 1911 *What Is and What Might Be*. London: Constable, 43

13 Widdows, G H 1910 'Derbyshire elementary schools: principles of planning'. *Royal Sanitary Institute Journal*, 92–116

14 Board of Education. Consultative Committee 1926 *The Education of the Adolescent* (Hadow Report). London: HMSO

15 Leathart, J 1940 'Current architecture'. *Building*, **15**, 208–9

16 Morris, H 1925 *The Village College: Being a Memorandum on the Provision of Education and Social Facilities for the Countryside with Special Reference to Cambridgeshire*. Cambridge: Cambridge University Press

17 Board of Education 1944 *Standard Construction for Schools* (Post-War Building Studies No 2). London: HMSO for Ministry of Works

18 Classey, E 1998, 'Fantastic Form – the Urban School; London's Comprehensive Schools 1950–1970', unpublished MSc, London University Bartlett School of Architecture

19 Planning Policy Guidance Note 15: 'Planning and the Historic Environment' (PPG15), paras 3.8 and 3.10. In 2010 this is set to be superseded by a Planning Policy Statement

Further reading

Châtelet, A-M, Lerch, D and Luc, J-N (eds) 2003 *Open Air Schools: An Educational and Architectural Venture in Twentieth-Century Europe* (text in French and English). Paris: Editions Recherches

Clark, C (ed England) and Seaborne, M (ed Wales) 1995 *Beacons of Learning: Urban Schools in England and Wales.* London: SAVE Britain's Heritage

Clay, Sir F 1929 *Modern School Buildings, Elementary and Secondary* (First pub 1902. 3 edn entirely rewritten). London: Batsford

Dent, H C 1970 *1870–1970: Century of Growth in English Education.* Harlow: Longman

Maclure, S 1984 *Educational Development and School Building, Aspects of Public Policy 1945–73.* Harlow: Longman

Orme, N 2006 *Medieval Schools: From Roman Britain to Renaissance England.* New Haven: Yale University Press

Robson, E R 1874 *School Architecture. Being Practical Remarks on the Planning, Designing, Building, and Furnishing of School-Houses.* London: Murray; facsimile reprint by Leicester University Press with an introduction by Malcolm Seabourne, 1972

Saint, A 1987 *Towards a Social Architecture: The Role of School Buildings in Post-War England.* New Haven and London: Yale University Press

Seaborne, M 1971 *The English School: Its Architecture and Organization*: *Vol I: 1370–1870.* London: Routledge & Kegan Paul

Seaborne, M and Lowe, R 1977 *The English School*: *Its Architecture and Organization: Vol II*: 1870–1970. London: Routledge & Kegan Paul

Selleck, R J W 1972 *English Primary Education and the Progressives, 1914–39.* London: Routledge & Kegan Paul

Weston, R 1991 *Schools of Thought: Hampshire Architecture 1974–1991.* Winchester: Hampshire County Council

Other titles in the Informed Conservation series

Behind the Veneer: The South Shoreditch furniture trade and its buildings.
Joanna Smith and Ray Rogers, 2006.
Product code 51204, ISBN 9781873592960

Berwick-upon-Tweed: Three places, two nations, one town.
Adam Menuge with Catherine Dewar, 2009.
Product code 51471, ISBN 9781848020290

The Birmingham Jewellery Quarter: An introduction and guide.
John Cattell and Bob Hawkins, 2000.
Product code 50205, ISBN 9781850747772

Bridport and West Bay: The buildings of the flax and hemp industry.
Mike Williams, 2006.
Product code 51167, ISBN 9781873592861

Building a Better Society: Liverpool's historic institutional buildings.
Colum Giles, 2008.
Product code 51332, ISBN 9781873592908

Built on Commerce: Liverpool's central business district.
Joseph Sharples and John Stonard, 2008.
Product code 51331, ISBN 9781905624348

Built to Last? The buildings of the Northamptonshire boot and shoe industry.
Kathryn A Morrison with Ann Bond, 2004.
Product code 50921, ISBN 9781873592793

Gateshead: Architecture in a changing English urban landscape.
Simon Taylor and David Lovie, 2004.
Product code 52000, ISBN 9781873592762

Manchester's Northern Quarter.
Simon Taylor and Julian Holder, 2008.
Product code 50946, ISBN 9781873592847

Manchester: The warehouse legacy – An introduction and guide.
Simon Taylor, Malcolm Cooper and P S Barnwell, 2002.
Product code 50668, ISBN 9781873592670

Margate's Seaside Heritage.
Nigel Barker, Allan Brodie, Nick Dermott, Lucy Jessop and Gary Winter, 2007.
Product code 51335, ISBN 9781905624669

Newcastle's Grainger Town: An urban renaissance.
Fiona Cullen and David Lovie, 2003.
Product code 50811, ISBN 9781873592779

'One Great Workshop': The buildings of the Sheffield metal trades.
Nicola Wray, Bob Hawkins and Colum Giles, 2001.
Product code 50214, ISBN 9781873592663

Ordinary Landscapes, Special Places: Anfield, Breckfield and the growth of Liverpool's suburbs.
Adam Menuge, 2008.
Product code 51343, ISBN 9781873592892

Places of Health and Amusement: Liverpool's historic parks and gardens.
Katy Layton-Jones and Robert Lee, 2008.
Product code 51333, ISBN 9781873592915

Religion and Place in Leeds.
John Minnis with Trevor Mitchell, 2007.
Product code 51337, ISBN 9781905624485

Religion and Place: Liverpool's historic places of worship.
Sarah Brown and Peter de Figueiredo, 2008.
Product code 51334, ISBN 9781873592885

Storehouses of Empire: Liverpool's historic warehouses.
Colum Giles and Bob Hawkins, 2004.
Product code 50920, ISBN 9781873592809

Stourport-on-Severn: Pioneer town of the canal age.
Colum Giles, Keith Falconer, Barry Jones and Michael Taylor, 2007.
Product code 51290, ISBN 9781905624362

Weymouth's Seaside Heritage.
Allan Brodie, Colin Ellis, David Stuart and Gary Winter, 2008.
Product code 51429, ISBN 9781848020085

£7.99 each (plus postage and packing)
To order through EH Sales
Tel: 0845 458 9910
Fax: 0845 458 9912
Email: eh@centralbooks.com
Online bookshop: www.english-heritageshop.org.uk